AF180380

TV is Not a Babysitter

Kyoko IWASA

TV is Not a Babysitter
Text © Kyoko IWASA 2022
The Japanese Edition Published in 1978 by Suiyosha Publishing Inc.

ISBN: 978-1-64273-204-7

No part of this may be reproduced or transmitted in any form or by any means, electronic or mechanical, including photocopying, recording, or by storage and retrieval system without the written permission of the publisher. For information contact the publisher. Every effort has been made to accurately present the work presented herein. The publisher and authors regret unintentional inaccuracies or omissions, and do not assume responsibility for the accuracy of the translation in this book. Neither the publishers nor the artists and authors of the information presented in herein shall be liable for any loss of profit or any other commercial damages, including but not limited to special, incidental, consequential or other damages.

Author: Kyoko IWASA
Projct Editor: Yumi Itabashi, Hachidori Inc.
Editor: Andrew Kirkham
Book Design: Lamplighters Label

Printed in USA
1 2 3 4 5 6 7 8 9 10

One Peace Books
43-32 22nd Street STE 204 Long Island City New York 11101
www.onepeacebooks.com

Synopsis

It is currently believed that autism is present since birth and cannot be treated, but I discovered a new theory. From the standpoint of Soviet psychology, I invented a new method of treatment. 10% of my worked cases have become "normal." But in Japan, my method is not approved and I have no heir.

Autism is considered a developmental disorder, but its cause is unknown.

I think that it is caused by excessive stimulation, like auditory stimulation and overconsumption of food. When exposed to overstimulation early in development, the brain becomes frantic, language cannot be understood properly, and speech is delayed.

In this book, I show the process of language development. When children stumble without progress, various symptoms of autism appear. I also show how to treat these children. Turn off the TV set for three years, do not give them much food, turn off the night light, and do not put them in group environments until two years after eliminating TV.

Furthermore, I will discuss how to approach kindergarten and how to approximate the mental age of autistic children based on their symptoms.

Finally, I will introduce real-world dialogue about autism treatment. "They will never be normal." If a child was born healthy and expected to be neurotypical, it is a tragedy to find out that they have become autistic. If they are under three years old, they have a chance at becoming normal.

KYOKO IWASA
21 May, 2022

Preface

Television is said to have spread to ninety-four percent of households in Japan today, with programs being broadcast from 6 AM to midnight. Young children and the elderly alike spend many hours every day in front of their screens. TV allows us to observe various scenes and events from all over the world. It enters deep into our lives as both a source of information and entertainment. Without TV, our lives would not be the same.

On the other hand, there has been a rise in the belief that "children these days can only focus for fifteen minutes," or that "television encourages passivity while extinguishing active, inquisitive minds." Recently, there have even been cases where three infants imitated scenes from a show and stomped, kicked, and killed a newborn baby, or a child jumping from the roof of a three-story building while reenacting TV and manga. Such instances have stirred up heated debates about the adverse effects of television on children. However, most of these discussions focus only on the content of television programs, speaking only of the negative influence of the shows themselves.

I have been conducting psychological evaluations for health examinations of three-year-old children since 1944. For infants and children, regardless of the content of the television programs, I feel there is an adverse effect that comes from the act of turning on the television itself.

Many mothers consider TV as a major source of information. They revel in their childhood memories of turning on the TV, laughing, and dancing along with the actors on the screen. TV teaches children what they can't, and when they're busy, TV keeps their children entertained. It is easy to imagine parents letting the TV "babysit their children." However, I have encountered several cases in which children who were brought up watching television in this way struggled with language development.

I came to wish from the bottom of my heart that this kind of attitude towards child rearing would be rectified. Whenever I tell someone, "If you keep the television on, your child's language development will be delayed," many people respond with "Really? Won't it help them learn words and everything else faster?" They look surprised or present a counterargument, but in reality, there is something wrong with this general belief.

Needless to say, words are used to convey our ideas to others and to our process thoughts. Words are a necessity. Because many children begin to talk when they reach a certain age, words are thought to be "produced" from within. However, words are actually the product of the people around them that work to help a child develop speech.

Without the efforts of others, normal language development is impossible. Not only that, as words are central to a child's cognitive development, delayed language development can lead to a delay in potty training. They may even have difficulties playing with other children. This can have lifelong effects, and in the worst case, can cause cognitive disabilities.

I have confirmed with my own eyes the relationship between delayed language development and television, and continue to commit myself to its evaluation and treatment. As a result, I am convinced that we cannot let TV babysit our children.

I wrote this little book in the hope of supporting parents who desire nothing but health and happiness for their child, for them to live a typical life without having to carry the burden of cognitive disabilities.

Table of Contents

Chapter 1

Meeting the Children

Unforgettable "U"

It was around 1970. I was conducting a psychological evaluation for three-year-old children at a public health center when, one day, I opened the door to a pretty little girl and her mother. The girl was endearing with short hair and red cheeks, and for a moment I wondered why this child had entered this room.

That is, not all children involved in medical examinations will end up in this room for psychological counseling. They only come if parents complain about some psychological problems such as bedwetting, thumb sucking, lack of social skills, and lack of appetite, or if a doctor or public health nurse decides that it is better for them to have a consultation.

Case U walked in through the door and onto the carpet with her shoes still on. "Shoes off," I said, but U completely disregarded my words and began to take out one toy after another. However, she did not take the toys to play with them. Instead, she took one and dropped it, took another and dropped that, repeating the same action in a steady motion.

She eventually went to the sink and, once realizing she could not reach, climbed onto a chair and turned on the faucet. With a great struggle, she sprayed the cleaner that was nearby, cleaned the sink with a sponge, and washed the grime away with water.

Once satisfied, she went to the gas stove and tried to twist the gas tap. I stopped her in a hurry, but thought I heard her say "Be careful when using gas..." or some kind of phrase from a TV commercial. I did not hear her clearly—maybe I had simply misheard her.

In this way, she continued to mouth words while picking up one thing after another, though I could not hear her say anything meaningful.

She eventually said "Potty" loudly, and her mom took her to the bathroom in a hurry. According to a public health nurse who observed them, even after coming out of the bathroom, the girl walked briskly along the corridor while facing straight forward. When the nurse offered her chocolate, she quickly took it and put it in her mouth. Her mother said she acted similarly at home, constantly moving and muttering. She was completely uninterested in her surroundings.

Personally, I was surprised as it was the first time I had met such a child who went around like this while murmuring without regard for their surroundings. I thought, "this is the autism that I read about in books," and introduced them to a municipal hospital known for its autism ward.

I waited a while for an update, but since I did not receive any, I asked a public health nurse to visit her house. According to the mother's story, they tried going to the municipal hospital, but since her daughter was still young, the doctors could not diagnose her with autism. It was decided they would monitor her in the meantime. The child went back to her usual ways, which often troubled the people around her. Eventually, she moved to Iwate Prefecture.

I do not know what became of her after that. I often remember U.

She should now be at an age to start elementary school, and I wonder a lot how she is doing, and whether she is going to school safely. I still do not know for certain whether U was autistic, but my encounter with U was a catalyst for me to become interested in these types of cases.

Until then, I worked with adult psychiatric patients suffering from mental illnesses, primarily those suffering from schizophrenia. Thus, examinations of three-year-old children was, so to speak, not my area of specialization.

To tell the truth, I was forced to do these examinations because I was asked to. In other words, because it was a part-time job rather than a full-time career, not only was I conscious of the fact that it was a part-time commitment, but it was full of things, such as about bedwetting, thumb-sucking, and delayed speech, I did not understand. My lack of capability often made me want to cry.

For the first time I understood the emotions of all the young mothers walking about with their child. Initially I did not know what to do, so I gave mothers an innocuous evaluation, only to go home and tear through relevant literature, keep track of each case, find some kind of pattern, and use that information to help the next child.

There are many cases in which children struggling with bedwetting and thumb-sucking get better from the age of four to five. Not only that, they have few problems from there on. But for children with language delays, my follow-up research has revealed bigger problems.

Even when language acquisition is slow, many children will be able to talk normally at around the age of three-and-a-half to four years old. However, some children do not speak even when they turn four or five years old. They are left behind at kindergarten and end up in facilities for children with learning disabilities, or are diagnosed with autism and begin receiving play therapy.

What an intricate issue. How can we tell which child is neurotypical at the age of three, and what kind of guidance should be given to children who are likely to have problems in the future?

"M" Who Grew Up Watching Television with Grandma

Sometime in January 1972, the pediatric department of the hospital where I was working at the time requested that I do an intelligence test on "M," an autistic child.

He was four years and eleven months old. As he entered the room he put his hands on everything, making it difficult to test him. I showed him pictures of a knife, scissor, desk, chair, horse, and cow, but he could not name any of them correctly. When counting Go stones he would say, "one, two, three… thirteen," but when asked how many there were in total, he could not understand. He pulled books off the shelves and twisted the faucets, constantly tinkering with something. "There goes Golden Bat!," "Hitachi Pana Color," "Zuzuzu ping pong papo," he would say, mimicking words and jingles I had often heard on TV.

I stopped the test and asked his mother how she raised him. His mom replied, "When he was born, his grandmother was still well. He was her first grandchild so she doted on him greatly and practically raised him herself. But when she got older, she watched TV all day long hugging him on her knee. She also loved to keep the house clean, so the neighbors' children were not allowed to come into the house and play. I didn't think that was good, but as her daughter-in-law, I could not push back. So, when I had my younger child, I took care of him. No matter how messy the house would get, I invited our neighbors' children over and let them play together. My younger child has just turned a year old, but he understands his surroundings better."

From the story of this mother and the state of the child, I thought that his symptoms may have something to do with the television he watched as a baby. As adults, we fully understand the images and sounds of the TV. But what about babies? What happens if a baby grows up in a room with the TV always on? That was the question that came to mind.

When I think about it, it seems that this encounter with M acted as a clue to my future research and practice regarding the influence of TV on the development of language in children.

"K" Who Calmed Down Without Television

After that at the public health center, we analyzed the evaluations and progress of three-year-old children with delayed speech and came to understand the following things.

Even if few words are uttered from the mouth of a child, those who give a clear reaction to the words directed at them usually catch up to other children by the age of four. But as for children who do not respond to their name; do not respond with an action to questions such as "Can you take off your shoes?," "Where is your mom?," or "Where is your tricycle?"; are able to answer the question "What is this?" but unable to choose correctly from a series of pictures when asked "Which is the scissor? Which is the pencil?"; these are the children who often have developmental concerns.

With such children, upon taking M's mother's experience as a hint, I started from 1973 to teach parents to turn off the TV entirely, talk to their children more, and take them out as much as possible to let them play with other children.

However, it is not easy at any household to completely eliminate television. Not many families did as I advised. Many of them figured children's shows were okay, or were told by other doctors that TV is irrelevant to their children's development and can be kept on.

Nevertheless, in September 1973, K returned to my examination room. Four months before, during his three-year medical checkup, he had been restless. He had hit the floor with a hammer, pulled the hair of another child until they cried, dropped a big box onto the feet of another child, and even rode a tricycle right out of the front gate. He had pushed away the language assessment picture book I tried to show him with a loud "No!" But his wild demeanor was gone. It is almost impossible to imagine that K had been so boisterous four months earlier. I heard him ask his mother, "Mom, can you buy me a book?" When I asked him who he came with, he answered, "With mama."

When he was riding the tricycle, I asked him to give it to the next child after a lap around the garden. To this, he did exactly as he was told and gave it to the next child.

He struggled to pronounce words, making it difficult to understand him at times. His speech was not smooth, and there were times when he would not understand my words. Still, compared to our first encounter four months earlier, he had made great progress.

I listened to his mother's story. After his three-year checkup, she had taken my advice and switched off the TV they had been watching for seven-and-a-half hours a day, as well as the records they had listened to for an hour each morning. She began seeing significant changes in K. He came to understand a lot of what his mother said, and he did not do violent things like before. But when interacting with kids of the same age, he often got into fights to get his own way. With that said, he got along with children who were bigger than him.

To be honest, I was still doubtful as to whether or not my

way was correct, but K's progress gave me great confidence. From then on, I started to give the same advice for similar cases like him.

Autism is Not an Emotional Disorder?

Through this process, I have learned autism may be found in children who struggle with delayed speech. I then had the question of how these children would develop as they grew older. I tried to read literature on this as well, but I decided it was better to check with my own eyes.

So, since 1973, I began visiting institutions for intellectually disabled infants, autism wards, kindergartens, schools for children with disabilities, and so on. In May 1973 I went to a private facility for intellectually disabled children under the jurisdiction of a public health center. It was a small facility of about thirty people. Most children commuted, but there was accommodation for those who lived farther away.

What grabbed my attention here was a fifteen-year-old boy who had been diagnosed with autism and frequented this facility since the age of five. In the garden, there was a trampoline on which little children were jumping. I saw a figure of a man crouching beside it. He watched the jumping children for a long time, and I thought he was a facility staff member. Eventually, he got up and came back into the room slowly, and he just stood without doing anything. He did not say anything when I talked to him. During snack time, he ate a rice cracker in silence and sometimes smiled. When it was time for cleaning, he brought a dustpan and swept the floor, but when he finished he began to hop around the room on both legs, indifferent to the other children.

His body was big for his age, and had I seen him from behind in a high school uniform, I would have thought him nothing more than a young student of seemly appearance… That was when tears filled my eyes. The appearance of such a boy was completely different from the image of autism I had before.

In general, autism is a type of emotional disorder (a disorder of the emotions), a child who shuts out the world without trying to interact with others because of an emotional trauma. There are few intellectual obstacles, and it was believed that the intellectual aspects would improve when the emotional aspects improved.

However, the demeanor of the boy who was said to be autistic was no different from that of patients suffering from severe mental disorders in a psychiatric hospital. I had worked at a mental hospital in Mitaka City with roughly 700 beds for about six-and-a-half years; the boy was in the same state as the severely mentally ill patients I saw there. The only difference was that he appeared physically strong.

I wondered if any of these children had been examined by me for their three-year checkup. As charming as they were as young children, their faces now showed little but blank emotion. It made me feel dejected. After that, I repeatedly visited facilities and schools here and there. I became increasingly unable to suppress the idea that autism is not simply a kind of emotional disorder, but rather a form of developmental disorder centered on intelligence.

Is Autism an Illness?

Ever since I published the first edition of this book, many mothers have asked me to examine their children. After much contemplation I quit my job in 1976, and in February of 1977, I opened the Luna Children's Consultation Office in Bunkyo Ward, Tokyo.

In July 1977 when I had started to fully devote myself to autism research, I was surprised to see "H" who had come from the Tohoku region for the first time in a while. Once again, he mouthed words from a commercial in a similar way to when he had eliminated TV a year ago, he was still unresponsive to me and, when outside, he preferred to roam about instead of holding my hand. In the beginning of April when he came here before starting kindergarten, he reacted to what his mother said and even composed two-word sentences like "Bake fish." When I took away his toy, he put his hands together and said, "Give me.".

To tell the truth, among the cases I have seen before, children who have experienced group settings such as kindergartens and nursery schools have more structured lifestyle habits compared to those who have received play therapy. They also begin to talk little by little, which is why I have always encouraged kids to enter kindergartens and nursery schools as early as possible.

H stopped watching TV when the one in his home broke in July 1976. After about six months, he stopped imitating commercials all day and began expressing demands. In April 1977, he was enrolled in a three-year kindergarten. Although I thought he would get better once he started kindergarten, H's condition worsened. When I asked his mother about his situation in kindergarten she said, "Since it is a large kindergarten, records play loudly in the mornings, teachers use microphones to speak to the children, and the radio is played on the bus." *But weren't these sounds detrimental to his development…?* I asked her to pull him out of the school for the time being.

Just when I thought he would improve in a quieter environment, his mother revealed that their family runs a store that faces a prefectural highway. Because of this, they are exposed to the sound of traffic all day long, with only about an hour of peace from 4 o'clock to 5 o'clock in the morning.

What to do…? Upon talking it over, H and his mother decided to go to a quiet hot spring in the mountains for about a month in mid-August. From the third week, he stopped imitating commercials and instead began speaking words such as "brother," "wiggle, wiggle (while looking at snakes)," and "bath." He began to settle down behaviorally as well. I did not expect that there would be a reversal or deterioration of autistic symptoms until I saw it in H.

As long as they learn words... as long as they can have conversations...

With autism being a developmental language disorder, I had assumed that symptoms would improve if the children became able to produce words on their own. But after seeing H get better and worse, autism seemed much more than a developmental language disorder.

Many children with autism struggle in the realm of language development, often repeating words spoken by others or talking to themselves. They may also speak differently than other children or not at all, not voicing a word even upon reaching the age of three or four despite not having any known hearing loss.

Some scholars believe that delayed speech is a cause of congenial defects of the brain, while others say it is the result of lack of bonding through physical contact as a baby. In this way, theories are varied.

I also jumped between different hypotheses. However, when I encountered the situation with H, I began to think that delayed language development in autistic children is not solely caused by insufficient communication from the people around them, but also by something in the child that makes them unreceptive to speech. That "something" will ameliorate if you reduce auditory stimulation and worsen if you increase it. If this "something" is in a good state the delayed language will also improve, but if it is not in a good state, speech will gradually disappear even with great effort. Even if it does not disappear completely, it may come out in the form of talking to oneself regardless of the surroundings, or in other ways that are not useful in terms of communication with others.

Seeing how symptoms fluctuate depending on the amount of auditory stimuli, it seemed that the cerebral cortex was out of order. If it could be returned to its normal state, I began to think that there would be improvements in the delay of language development. Though I felt bad for H, worsening symptoms simultaneously indicated the possibility of making them better. H's case not only helped me come to this realization, but also deepened my awareness about autism.

Chapter 2

Process of Acquiring Language and Its Stagnation

The age of infancy from around zero to one year old is a time of considerable development of the body, so the concerns of the people around babies are also directed towards their weight, first steps, and other physical aspects of their growth. Regarding mental development, we also tend to pay attention to *what* our babies did, whether it is laughing, saying "mama" and so on.

But I took a step further and began considering what kind of actions are made in order to make a baby laugh, or whether their reaction differs when the mother speaks or when the television speaks. I thought it necessary to look more closely at the interactions between children and their surroundings.

Furthermore, in treating autistic children, I sought clarity in how language acquisition takes place and at which points of development autistic children tend to stumble. To do so, I devoured literature on these topics and analyzed the various symptoms that manifest in children.

However, there are many studies about speech in children. Some dictate that infants begin babbling two to three months after birth, or that they will begin talking when they are one year old. Nonetheless, there are few studies on the process of how children become able to understand the words of the people around them.

Neurotypical children generally understand the meanings of the words they speak. Thus, studying the words they use will often suffice. But with autistic children, even if they can imitate phrases from a commercial, they may not understand the question, "Where is your mom?" It became imperative to meet head-on the issues revolving around the processes of language acquisition and comprehension.

Therefore, I thought about how to proceed in understanding the development of children's speech. I proceeded to combine the various patterns of speech in autistic children with the Soviet study of developmental psychology and Pavlov's second signal system.

This is what I will discuss in this chapter.

Language is the core of human spiritual activity, and if the development of language is bad, it can negatively affect our intelligence and development, as well as the emotional and social aspects of our lives.

Does Your Baby Like TV?

I once came across a contribution in a newspaper: "My first-born son who I gave birth to last year has been watching TV since he was one month old, and I'm quite concerned. At first, I thought he took interest in the glowing images on the screen. When he was two or three months old, I sat him in a chair and placed him a few meters away from the TV. He squealed with happiness. After that, it became common for him to watch for over an hour at a time…"

Even such a small baby will react when watching TV, and this often propels parents to willingly let them watch television. But do babies really understand what they watch on TV?

Are they really squealing with joy? It all seems rather dubious. That's because it is. This is just a reflex.

After about two weeks from birth, a baby will show an automatic reaction to a loud sound. At three weeks to five weeks, they will turn their head towards something shiny. In technical terms, this is called an orienting reflex and is an immediate response to changes in the outside world.

As the TV screen is always switching to new images and emitting various sounds, the baby will display an orienting reflex in reaction to that change. This makes babies appear as though they are engrossed in watching TV.

However, an orienting reflex towards sound and light plays a very important role in learning words.

Although it will be a little technical, let's look at this step by step.

First Stage: Understanding Voices

When a baby is born, you must first give it milk. If you repeatedly give milk while saying, "Now, let's have some milk," the word "milk" and the action of drinking it become linked in the baby's mind. This is an unconditioned response to food which is present from the time of birth. It is the same response that makes babies suck on things that touch their lips or swallow anything that reaches the depths of their mouth. Besides this, if they are repeatedly spoken to when being hugged, held, or having their diapers changed, the baby will gradually show distinct reactions to the human voice.

At first, babies demonstrate auditory unconditioned response to the sound of a door closing, the wind, the clinking of utensils, and a plethora of other noises. Whatever the sound, they will turn their head towards it. Gradually, they'll begin to understand that a person's voice is often a precursor for a reward such as milk or a cuddle, while other sounds are not. Soon they will start to respond to voices, but not to other general noises unless they are extremely loud.

Auditory unconditioned response is said to be "complete" when the ability to distinguish between voices and other sounds has been established. According to the studies of developmental psychology in the Soviet Union, this is believed to take about four to five months after birth.

In order for human beings to acquire language, it is more important than anything to be able to distinguish the voices of people. But severely autistic children often elicit little to no response when spoken to, and some children can only engage in vocal stimming. In these cases, I feel that their development may have stopped at this stage.

On the premise of the above explanation, please think about cases in which babies are left in a room with a TV for a long time. You can presume that the babies have become accustomed to the sound of TV.

It is easy to imagine that the auditory unconditioned response towards human voices has not been formed.

Adults can distinguish between the sound of TV and real-life conversations. So, even in a room with a TV, it is possible to have a conversation that is irrelevant to what is being shown on the screen.

However, babies who have not memorized words yet cannot tell the difference between the sound of TV and real-life conversation. Every sound is absorbed without the knowledge of what is important and what is not. Since the volume of a TV is usually not so different from the volume of a human voice, children raised in a room with a TV can become insensitive to the human voice. Even if others talk to them in respect to their behavior, the words do not link in their mind and do not lead to true language acquisition.

When I listen to stories about children who are thought to be autistic, I am often told that they were quiet, unresponsive to attempts at communication, or were thought to have hearing loss. Such reactions are typically seen around four to six months after birth, but the fact that this was not the case suggested a delay in development.

Considering that the presence of these reactions creates the basis of subsequent language development, you can imagine how harmful TV can be for a baby when they are exposed to it for long periods.

Second Stage: Distinction by Intonation

About four months after birth, babies will be able to distinguish between human voices and other sounds. But at this stage, the content of what is being talked about is irrelevant. This is because sound differentiation has not been acquired yet.

If distinguishing human voices from other sounds is the first step, distinguishing the intonation of words is what appears to be the second. Every time we play "peek-a-boo!" or "up, up and away!" with children, we all talk to them in a friendly, playful way. When trying to stop a child who is about to fall from a landing or touch a hot stove, we naturally say "No! It's dangerous!" in a loud voice. The tone of our voices is completely different.

Even if a child cannot fully make out our words, it remembers the connection between the situation and intonation from the power and emotion of the words and the stimulus to their body that follows. Of course, it cannot yet imitate that intonation, but it seems that the foundation of correct intonation will be created at this stage in their childhood.

With an autistic child who can speak to a certain extent, it is common that their intonation does not match the situation they are in. Usually, there is a rise in pitch at the end of a question, while demands are spoken in a firmer, lower pitch.

In the case of an autistic child, their demands might be spoken like a question, or they might speak in a high, monotonous tone. When they want something, they might say in a high, flat voice, "Tell me what you want," or, "Milk?," mimicking the way a mother speaks to her child. They might also make demands like "Potty!" or "Cookie!" while looking in a completely different direction. Even if their words are appropriate for the situation, it often happens that their intonation is not. When asked "What is this?," they might answer by repeating the same exact words.

Children begin to talk when they are older, but as you can see in the examples above, it is possible that autistic children already show symptoms of delayed language development at the age of five to six months when other neurotypical children may already be learning how to differentiate between various intonations.

Third Stage: Phonological Distinction

Once babies are able to distinguish voices and noise, intonations, and whether they are being scolded or played with, they will gradually begin to understand what adults are saying to them. An important factor that promotes this understanding is eye and hand movement. With this, babies can start to hear different phonemes (A, B, C).

About four months after birth a baby can follow people and objects with their eyes, but cannot keep its focus on one thing for long or look at things with a sense of curiosity. But from this stage onwards a baby will increasingly start using its hands and, at about five months after birth, will be able to grab things. Once able to grasp objects, they will quickly learn how to match their eye and hand movements. They will move their hands to grab something, and eventually begin to stare at them.

At around six months old, they will not only sleep but start turning over and trying to sit. They will move their bodies around and begin to grab a wider range of objects in their immediate surroundings. They will extend their hands, grab and drop objects, give hugs, and deepen their interactions with adults. They will enjoy being spoken to and start understanding verbs like "be," "not be," "fall," and "hug." Learning nouns such as "mama," "milk," and "toy" becomes much more rapid when babies can closely focus on individual objects and become able to clearly recognize them.

At first, the eyes can only distinguish between bright or dark. However, shape recognition develops from about 3 months old, soon after which babies will be able to distinguish objects from their backgrounds. When they are repeatedly exposed to the same shape or a shape with special significance, recognizing it will become even easier.

The first thing that leaves an impression in a baby's mind is the face of a human being. Around four months after birth, most babies will perceive faces and begin smiling. They are more likely to smile at someone who talks to them as opposed to someone who remains silent.

At around the age of five months, the orienting reflex described earlier also appears in vision, and babies begin to reach out at any new object they find. Whether it is a toy, cup, or the lid of a cooking pan, a baby will grab whatever it can, examine it, and play with it for a while. If an adult comes by to say, "Here's your toy, can you hear it rattling?," or "Let's go wash your hands!," the baby will connect what it saw, the actions it made with its hands, and the words spoken to it by the grownup. This is how words are formed as an orienting reflex.

From around six months old, babies begin to yearn for the affection of adults in particular. They will reach their hands out if an adult passes by, and if ignored, will cry and make noises to try and get their attention. They will laugh with joy when an adult plays with them, and will start to make various sounds with their voice.

From about two months after birth, a baby will begin to babble words like "ah" or "ooh." But if an adult responds with, "Ah, what's wrong?," or "Ooh, you want water?," the baby will become more and more talkative.

By making a sound, listening to its own voice, and having an adult repeat the sound, the act of speaking will be further strengthened. In this way, babies begin to understand words through interactions with adults by creating connections between what it sees, what it feels with its body, and the words it hears.

As babies approach the age of one, they will start responding appropriately to various phrases: looking at their father when asked, "Where's daddy?," giving an adult the object in their hand after being asked, "Can I have that?," or quickly pulling their hand away when someone says, "No, that's dangerous!"

As I have demonstrated above, I think it is quite obvious

that exchanges with adults are very important for the comprehension of language in children. But such interactions do not necessarily have to be had with the mother. As long as they are sensitive to the baby's interests, expressions, and movements and respond appropriately through verbal and physical contact (hugging, cuddling), neighbors, nannies, and anyone else who will actively interact with the baby is OK. This is why I ask parents to create opportunities for their children to interact with many adults.

However, with autistic babies, I often hear concerns of them not smiling when played with, not making eye contact, or not shying away from anyone they meet. Usually when you play with a baby, you speak to it directly. But with autistic babies, because the orienting reflex towards voices has not been formed, the baby does not turn to the sound of the voice. It will not meet your gaze, the cognition of the adult's face will be delayed, and it will not laugh even if you play with it. Even towards the mother, a baby might not laugh nor show any other signs of recognition. In such cases, attempts to play with the baby might prove rather disappointing.

One of the greatest motivations for adults to play with babies is receiving a response, a giggle or squeal when they are tickled or picked up. With no reaction at all, it can be difficult to try to keep the communication going. Therefore, it is thought that babies who are quiet and unresponsive will fall into a vicious circle in which the chances of them being spoken to diminish, causing further delay in language development.

Furthermore, usually from the seventh to eighth month after birth, shyness begins to develop. When a stranger holds their hands out, a baby might turn away. Or, when meeting someone for the first time, it might look at their face for a while before crying. However, many autistic babies do not show these types of reactions. They will not mind being held by anyone. Because they cannot properly recognize faces, it is difficult for them to distinguish a stranger from an acquaintance, suggesting a delay in their cognitive development. Recognition of the faces and voices of others and laughter during playtime are indispensable elements to the baby's acquisition of language and their interactions with other people. In this process, the baby learns to look at the people around them and gaze at objects in their hand, deepening their understanding of the world around them.

However, with autistic children, this understanding can be delayed because there is little interaction with other people. Even at three to four years old, there are quite a few children who do not have the same level of language development as a neurotypical one-year-old. Even while saying "bye-bye," the baby may not turn towards the other person. When asked, "Where is your mom?," the child may not turn to its mother. Some children do not understand the words "Let's go home," leading to mothers dragging their hands as if to pull a dog.

Once they start elementary school, while they might be able to say "Watch out, a car's coming!," when others say "Stop at the red light!," they might not understand. In this way, comprehension of others' words is lower by several steps than of words that come out of their own mouth.

As children get older, the number of words they express may increase slightly. But even then, comprehension will not be quite as smooth. Even if they can answer yes or no questions such as "Do you have a toy truck at home?" or "How about dolls?," they may not know how to answer questions like "What other kinds of toys do you have?"

In this way, it can be difficult to grasp the concept of "toy" under which lie trucks and dolls. They can also struggle with spatial awareness such as "lowering down" their pants or turning "backwards." Upon being shown pictures of a bird and car and asked "Which one flies in the sky? Which one runs on roads?," they may not be able to answer. They will also lack the ability to grasp functional concepts that are invisible to the eye.

Fourth Stage: Comprehension Through Experience

From about seven to eight months after birth, the baby will hold onto objects in an attempt to stand up and walk, crawl on all fours, and expand its range of movement. The biggest change comes when they begin to walk on their own.

Children nowadays grow up fast with some walking as early as ten months old. On average, most will start walking at around the age of one or one year and two months. Standing up after months of lying down and sitting completely changes a child's view of the world. This is because the position of the eyes become much higher. Walking further alters the perspective of a child.

Even when walking while thinking that nothing is wrong, they might stumble on a toy, get caught on a table cloth and trigger a rain of items to fall on their head, or be scolded after climbing up on the *kotatsu* (heated table). Everything that had seemed harmless when they could only sit still will suddenly seem to jump back at them. When they experience burns, pain, surprise, and sadness, an adult will come running and say, "Pain, pain, go away! Did you trip on this rock?" and so on.

For the child, each action is new and kindles curiosity towards various aspects of their life. They cannot help but reach for one thing after another. Through being scolded or experiencing surprise, the baby will notice that one thing appears to take various shapes, or that another object is called by different names. The shape of a cup is completely different when seen from above and from the side, but adults will always say, "Here's your cup." Alternatively, when they say, "Here's your snack," they might serve anything from wafers to oranges.

At this juncture, children do not fully understand the correlation between words and objects. They understand by sensing the overall atmosphere of the situation and the adult's words, blending it all together through their own eyes, ears, tongue, skin, and motions.

When a child sees an adult petting a dog while saying "Look at the big doggy," "What a cute doggy!," or "The doggy's going to sleep, say 'night, night,'" they will only really pick up the repeated word "doggy." Looking at the four-legged animal and hearing the word "doggy" repeated again and again, petting them, waving at them, and watching them stretch and yawn, the children will slowly come to recognize that the moving thing in front of them is "doggy." The other words such as "big," "cute," and "sleep" are mere accessories to "doggy," and are not yet understood clearly. It is not until they hear other phrases such as "big balloon" that the word "big" will really start to come alive.

At this stage, words alone are not enough for the child to comprehend the situation. Actions are needed to supplement the words. If an adult asks, "Can I have that?" while putting out their hand, the child will either hand the object in their hand or hold it tighter to refuse. But if the request is only verbal, they might simply stare while wondering what was said.

To explain in slightly difficult terms, situations and actions are called the first-signal system in terms of conditioned response. This first-signal system refers to everything that has various implications and influences our behavior. It means that if you put out both hands in front of a child, they know you are suggesting that they give you something, or that if a person waves, they will soon be gone. Even without words, children will begin to understand these situations when they are repeated several times. Conditioned response is believed to be formed with this ability to understand.

When words such as "Give me" and "bye-bye" are repeated together with the first signal of situations and actions, the correlation between the situations and words is made. Children will be able to predict that the other person will put out their hand whenever they say "Can I have that?," or that they will wave if they say "bye-bye." Words like "Give me" and "bye-bye" work as a signal of such behavior, which is why from here on we will refer to words as a "second-signal system." or the "signal of a signal." This was the term created by the Russian physiologist Ivan Pavlov.

Even if language comprehension begins, until about one and a half years old, children are still in the stage where the relationship between the first-signal system (real-life stimuli) and the second-signal system (words) is being created. The second-signal system alone is not enough to fully evoke the first-signal system. Understanding comes only with the simultaneous presence of the first-signal system.

This stage is also one in which children begin to learn meaningful words. However, due to the still underdeveloped vocal organs and lack of practice, only a few words can be pronounced and long conversations are impossible. It is a stage of single-word sentences such as "mama," "water," or "car."

In this way, since the first words that are learned are single words, it seems as if comprehension begins from individual words to longer sentences. But in reality, it is the opposite. The child witnesses an event and hears the words uttered by the adult, absorbing them as whole phrases. They gradually notice that some words are repeated in various situations and develop the ability to consciously separate those words from the others.

Through this process, the abstraction of words is also understood. They capture not just what is in front of them, but the essence functional aspects that exist in its depth. Although it all sounds rather difficult, to put it simply it is something like the following: Returning to the example of "doggy," adults will call their own dog "doggy," or say "Here comes a doggy" as they point to one during an afternoon stroll. They will see a white Spitz and say "Cute doggy," while they might call a big, growling German Shepherd a "scary doggy." Though they vary in shape and size, whether it is their own dog or their neighbor's, they will repeatedly call those barking, four-legged creatures "doggy." With this repetition, children will begin to link the four-legged animals to "doggy," transcending the specific qualities of the dog in front of them. Being able to conjure a general image of dogs irrespective to the one they see in front them is the key to developing from the first-signal system to the second-signal system.

By grasping the "abstraction" and "generalization" of words, it becomes possible to notice commonalities among various things, make abstract the parts that are not essential, and understand the various properties of the real world. This is the first step in thinking with words.

So, at this stage, it is important to let children have as many experiences as possible and for adults to stand close by to help express those experiences in words. Even if a child touches everything in sight while experiencing pain and surprise, if it is not expressed in words, the experience will stay at the level of the first-signal system. It will not develop into the second-signal system of abstraction and generalization.

Although dogs and dolphins can understand human language and learn tricks, it is only up to the level of one-and-a-half-year babies in which the first-signal system and second-signal system act in conjunction. There is no way for them to reach the next level of thought which uses only the second-signal system.

It is well known that language distinguishes animals from humans, but in a strict sense, it is safe to say that human beings become human beings for the first time by acquiring this second-signal system. So, at the age of about one-and-a-half years, neither human intelligence nor a chimpanzee's intelligence are qualitatively different.

Compared to those with severe autism who are barely responsive and know almost no words, some autistic children have a first-signal system of the same level as intelligent animals, allowing them to reach the a level of language development equivalent to one-and-a-half-year-olds.

When told "Time to eat" they will sit at the table, and when plates are brought out they will go get their eating utensils. When the mother says "We're going shopping" they will walk to the front door and put on their shoes. In this way, habitual behavior can be established, making parents believe that they are not so developmentally behind because they can understand what they say.

However, these verbal interactions are often accompanied by a first signal such as food or shopping baskets, so even if the words are not understood, appropriate actions can be taken. However, this only indicates that the conditioned response for the first-signal system has been completed. This alone is insufficient.

In the case of autistic children, since the communication between the first-signal system and the second-signal system is not seamless, even if they hear words (second-signal system), they cannot form a mental picture of what the word is actually indicating (first-signal system). For that reason, even if they can repeat the words, concrete understanding does not follow.

Normally, the mother's existence and the word "mama" are equivalent. If a child is told "I hate you!," the child will become very quiet to avoid being disliked by their mother. But with autistic children, even if they hear the word "mama," they do not know who that is, or whether it is a person or an object. They simply put on a vacant look. With other autistic children, when asked "What is this?," they can answer correctly like "apple" or "car." However, when asked "Which is an apple?," or "Which is a car?," they will not understand at all.

In other words, it is very difficult to return from the second-signal system to the first-signal system, even though you can transpose from the first-signal system to the second-signal system. The first-signal system is also in animals, and it acts in the baby soon after it is born.

Conditioned response is created first in the first-signal system. After it is fully formed, it is then created in the second-signal system. The route from the first-signal system to the second-signal system is relatively clear. But the route from the second-signal system to the first-signal system is not seamless if the route from the first-signal system to the second-signal system has not been solidly formed. As the connection between the first-signal system and the second-signal system is being created, abstract action as an important function of words is also created at the same time.

In the example of "doggy" mentioned earlier, the white Spitz in front of the child is the first signal, and the word "doggy" is the second signal. The neighbor's bulldog is also a first signal, and it is also called "doggy." In this way, disparate first signals are often expressed in the second signal by using the same word. In order to be able to recognize this relationship, the child will first have to connect both the Spitz and the bulldog (first signal) to the word "doggy" (second signal). Upon hearing "doggy," they must be able to conjure images of both a Spitz and a bulldog.

However, in the case of autistic children, the association between the first-signal and the second-signal is weak. They tend to lack the ability to grasp the essence of things, to strip away unnecessary details to form a more abstract image in their minds.

In addition, communication by words is possible because

words as the second-signal system bring about common recognition. But for autistic children, this common recognition is often difficult. Because grasping the commonly recognized first signal is difficult, communication often does not go well.

As a characteristic of children with autism, they are often able to express requests such as "juice" or "cracker" but are unresponsive to the words of others. In this case, the desire to have juice or a cracker falls on the first signal, and the second signal are the corresponding words. Thus, by saying "juice" or "cracker," the people around them understand what they want.

But still, the opposite is not true. They might be asked, "Do you want juice or milk?," a question to which they cannot form an answer. So when communicating with an autistic child, the conversation is often one way instead of a back-and-forth.

Fifth Stage: Increased Chatter

From around one year old, children start speaking simple sentences. Unlike babbling, these are short phrases that contain meaning for adults. They start with words that are easy to pronounce such as "mama" or "doggy." "Mama" might not necessarily indicate their mother, and may just be a way to call others close or a way to signify they are hungry. Sometimes it is hard to know what the child means until we see the actions that supplement their words.

Furthermore, depending on the situation in which they

learned a word, they may also show incorrect usage. For example, in a household where the father is rarely at home, a child may point at a picture of a man in a newspaper and say "Daddy," even after being shown a picture of their own father before that. Even when shown a landscape picture, they might say "Daddy." Far from the parent's intention, the child in this instance has taken the word "daddy" to mean "photograph." Similarly, they might say "doggy" whether they are looking at a dog, cat, or lion.

At this stage, since there is no connection between objects and words yet in the real sense, if they find something unusual, they might point and say "Ah… ah…!" While that is a rather ordinary way to draw the attention of adults, they might instead say something like "Mama... mommy" or "Meow… cat!" Adults will be delighted that they have spoken words, and, seeing their joy, the children become increasingly willing to use them.

These insufficient expressions and mistaken use of words are often the cause of underdeveloped vocal organs or lack of practice, but they also have the following cause.

By this time, children can see clearly and sufficiently distinguish between objects and their backgrounds. But the overall impression comes first, and the eyes do not reach the point where they can process details.

Parts that leave the most impression in their minds at that particular time end up being associated with the words used in that situation. If an adult happens to say "Hot! Don't touch!"

when a child accidentally touches the stove, they might later look at it and say "Hot! Hot!," even when it isn't. Unable to make the distinction between the words "water" and "milk," they might ask for "water" when they actually want milk, ultimately getting angry when they are given water. This can be expressed as the "inability to differentiate concepts."

From around a year and a half, the number of learned words further increases. Expressions become quite concrete, like "Doggy come.," "Want cake.," "Mama give me.," or "Hand dirty." When it reaches this stage, it is possible to understand a child's request without having to look directly at them.

However, even in this case, further observation will reveal that they are often pointing at something directly in front of them and calling its name, or voicing requests associated with a physical or psychological need such as wanting to drink, eat, and play. Just like seeing a train and saying "train," hiding from a big dog and saying "scary," expressing hunger with the words "want food," or saying "Out, out" when eager to play outside, the words are always accompanied by the presence of a first signal.

Also during this period, children begin to increasingly imitate and repeat the words they hear. "What is this?," they might say while pointing to what is in front of them. After seeing the adults they are mimicking joyfully answer, they will start to repeat the phrase over and over again.

There are cases where the child will ask this question about something they really do not understand, but otherwise it is half play—they are simply repeating, or are asking even if they already know the answer. Also, they will often imitate what strangers say. If someone happens to say, "So you're not going to continue?," they might repeat "continue?..." or if another person says "I don't care about that," they might say, "don't care." This tendency to mimic is quite evident when playing with children around one to two years old.

When an older child says "I'm here," they will repeat the same words. If they hear another child shouting "Breaking news! Breaking news!" while playing, they will copy everything from their gestures to intonation. They can go on like this for thirty minutes or even an hour until they are finally scolded by an adult. Even when counting "1, 2, 3, 4, 5...," they are usually mouthing the words without understanding the concept of numbers. As evidence, many children will hand over one, perhaps three building blocks when asked for two.

As mentioned earlier, the words entering their ears come as fully formed sentences, so once their vocal organs develop, the phrases they say will also be longer.

Traditional methods of categorizing language as single-word sentences, two-word sentences, and three-word sentences simply apply the adult concept of speech to the vocabulary of children. In the case of children, they do not say phrases like "Doggy come" with the intention of combining a noun (doggy) with a verb (come). When an adult sees a dog walking towards them they say, "Look, here comes the doggy."

At first, children have weak memory and have difficulty remembering whole sentences. They also have trouble pronouncing sounds. However, their manner of speaking gradually becomes closer to that of adults as they become able to learn longer phrases and enunciate words. Expressions relating to their current needs or what is in front of them are all on the same level. Phrases like "Food.," "Food yummy.," and "More food." are all the same in that the first-signal system and the second-signal system coexist.

However, being able to talk in this way is very important in reinforcing the words they hear by ear. This is because in order to talk, the vocal organs including the lips, tongue, and throat must be exercised in complex ways. It is the cerebral voluntary motor cortex that is responsible for this movement, and it is located from the top of the head to the ear. This motor cortex can retain a remarkably larger amount of information than the visual or auditory cortex, and it does not easily forget that which was once committed to memory. It is the same as how the ability to swim or ride a bicycle does not fade even after a decade.

In this way, children memorize language by connecting the words they hear with information they absorb through their eyes, hands, and mouth, and reinforcing those words through vocal repetition The number of words learned from age one to around one-and-a-half increases gradually, but from a year-and-a-half to around two years the number will increase rapidly. Because being able to speak means communication with others is possible, the world will suddenly seem bigger for children. Though they previously had no other means but to cry or hit something they did not like, they become able to express their feelings by saying "No!," "Go away!," or "Don't like!"

Furthermore, from the adult's perspective, while they had had to judge their child's comprehension by examining their behavior, they eventually become able to do so by listening to what they say. This makes it easier for them to interact with their children because they will know whether they understand and are using the words they've learned correctly. In this way, through communication with adults, children memorize words and deepen their understanding of the world around them.

Autistic children also begin to imitate words as commonly seen with neurotypical children their age, but their manner of speaking is slightly different. The most common case is said to be "parroting." For example, if a waiter says "Welcome," the child will also say "Welcome" while entering the restaurant. Or, when asked "Who did you come with?," they will repeat, "Who did you come with?," exactly as they had heard. There were children whose mothers waited expectantly for them to start speaking, only to find that at the age of two they would only repeat the words they heard. Some would even continue this "parroting" until they were around five to seven years old.

Similar to this, there is what is called delayed echolalia. This is when a series of words spoken in a past situation is repeated in exactly the same way in a later situation. The words are not modified to fit the latter situation, so even though they may speak longer phrases, the meaning is unclear.

For example, a typically quiet three-and-a-half-year-old would suddenly say at lunch time, "So, what should I make today? Fried rice? Or maybe omurice? ," just like their mother. "To be honest, it always makes me laugh.," the mother told me with a sheepish smile. Of course, the words themselves were correct and were being pronounced rather well. However, this was just an imitation of the mother and not the words that children usually speak. Usually they will say, "I want omurice!" or "Make me fried rice!" To imitate the mother only indicates that the situation, their mother, and the words spoken at the time were absorbed and fed back out again exactly as they were seen and heard.

*(Note: **Omurice** is a popular Japanese dish that is an omelette made with fried rice and thin, fried scrambled eggs, usually topped with ketchup.)*

The function of words within a second-signal system to understand the situation, connect it with the words of their mother, and assess the situation in relation to themselves is non-existent. This is consistent with the explanation above. The fixed scene as the first-signal system and the word as the second-signal system are committed to memory undifferentiated. When the children find themselves in the same situation as before, they only recall the phonetic aspect of the second-signal system and vocalize that. In the case of parroting, the words will be repeated on the spot, but with delayed echolalia they are more likely to be repeated after a certain period of time.

However, since there is no effort to understand the meaning of the words and convey intentions, even if long phrases can be spoken with accurate pronunciation, we cannot expect much development from there on out.

Similar to this, there are autistic children who have memorized numerous commercials or can sing songs very well. As their enunciation is decent and the melodies are sung accurately, it can seem strange that they struggle to learn ordinary words. However, if we hypothesize that this is also a kind of delayed echolalia, the mystery can be easily solved.

Indeed, commercials convey meaning, and if you hear a child mimicking a commercial, it would seem as if they understand its content well. But, like a tape recorder, it is also possible that they are simply imitating. Even if the commercial is quite long, if they hear it several times a day, it is no wonder that they can remember it in its entirety and repeat it.

The same is true for songs. Melodies must be memorized as they are and the lyrics do not necessarily have to be understood. It is the same as how some children can sing well in English without knowing what they are singing. Because Japanese children mostly sing Japanese songs, adults tend to assume that they have a level of comprehension in regards to the lyrics they sing.

In the case of autistic children, no matter if they can sing an entire song or repeat a long commercial, that is that, and developing their language to the point where they are able to have conversations is a wholly different matter.

Sixth Stage: Recalling Words

There is no clear distinction between each stage of language acquisition as described so far, save for the very first stage of the distinction between voices and sounds. Other stages of language development will blur together or proceed in parallel with each other.

The formation of the following concepts is also the same. Unless children become able to distinguish between voices and sounds (first stage), it is impossible to proceed to the following stages of differentiating intonations and achieving general comprehension. Therefore, the presence or absence of response to voices has a decisive influence on the development of subsequent words.

However, if this response is present the subsequent stages will complement each other and develop even if there is some imbalance, although it might be more appropriate to say "reinforce" rather than "complement."

The next significant step is the formation of "conceptualization."

Every time a child finds something or performs various actions, the people around them speak to them. They even begin to imitate their words. When they encounter similar situations they repeat the action of vocalizing words, in turn making stronger connections between the scenes and relevant vocabulary. Simultaneously, they will begin to understand that many of the same words are used in various situations. As they learn to do the same, the conceptualization of those words will be completed. For example, the word "mama" is used to indicate their mother, but other children also use the word "mama" to call their own mothers. When calling the mother of another child, they would not say "mama." Instead they will call them "auntie" or "so-and-so's mom." And when they talk about that "aunt," they will have to say "that auntie" or "so-and-so's mom."

In other words, they must be able to distinguish between their own and other children's mothers, and understand that their relationship with their mother also exists between other children and their mothers. If a child points to a woman other than their mother and says "Mama," points to someone else when asked "Where is your mom?," or sees a baby and says "Mom," that signifies their lack of comprehension. No matter who says "mama," the child must be able to discern the meaning of the word and use it accordingly towards their own mother and the mothers of other children. Only then, for the first time, it can be considered that the concept of the word "mama" has been understood.

The same also applies to verbs. They must learn to say "Give me cake," "Give me water," or "Give me bread." When told to "Bring newspaper," "Bring chopsticks," or "Bring a rag," they must be able to bring the items even if they are not in front of them. Whatever other words are pronounced alongside the learned words, it is important that they can understand correctly and take the appropriate actions. It is necessary for them to know how to use the verbs as pertaining to themselves, as well as to anything else around them. It is also common to see misused words like "Grill milk!" This, however, is in a sense the efforts of a thinking child. It is a positive step forward in the developmental process, that is, the stage of conceptualization.

Namely, they listen to words such as "grill fish" or "grill meat" and reason that placing something over fire to heat it is to "grill." They will then immediately try using their newly learned word as in "grill milk." Since adults do not say "Let's grill milk," it is clear that the child selected the word "grill" through their own thought processes. Unfortunately, they could not distinguish between solids and liquids. Therefore, they said "grill" instead of "boil."

In this way, the second phase of distinguishing intonations to the fifth phase was always in coexistence with the first-signal system, whereas the sixth stage of the formation of concepts is the first step beyond dependency on the first-signal system and towards language that functions within the second-signal system. This is very important.

In fact, this function of the second-signal system, that is, whether the use of conceptualized words is successful or not, is the second fork in the road as to whether or not subsequent language development will be smooth. Once children are able to use words as concepts, their ability to talk will quickly become enhanced.

At first, children babble. From there they begin saying short sentences like "This is a demon. Scary," or "I'm scared, the ghost is coming," while looking at a picture book. They might also say phrases such as "I give you tea., "Spoon too." Or "Please!" As they engage in longer conversations while talking and playing, they will become increasingly conscious of others when taking actions and speaking.

("Birth of Words" Japan Broadcasting Publishing Association)

Until this stage the first-signal system was always an intermediary, creating one-way interactions from adult to child or from child to adult. When a child says "Fish, fish!" while pointing to a picture in a book, the parent will answer with "Yes, it's a big fish." The child will then move on to point to another thing, repeating this one-way interaction.

When it comes to the formation of concept, the child will respond directly to the words of the other person.

"Do you want to go potty, Betty?"

"No."

"Are you embarrassed?"

"I wet my pants."

"When did you wet your pants?"

"When I was playing."

("Birth of Words" Japan Broadcasting Publishing Association)

As such, the exchange of adults → children → adults → children will become possible. In fact, some children will be able to engage in such complete conversations from around two-and-a-half to three years old. Before they can participate in such conversations, others will struggle to organize their thoughts and may go to adults and repeat words like "Say, say," or "Now, now."

There might be a period when they cannot conjure the rest of their sentences, or talk at length using completely incomprehensible sentences. Some children go through a period where they cannot be understood by anybody when speaking phrases longer than three words. This often happens when they want to tell others what they have experienced, not when they are talking about their needs or thoughts of that moment. In these situations, they are trying to step outside the realm of coexistence with the first-signal system and enter the realm of only the second-signal system. However, they get stuck because the second-signal system is still incomplete.

However, if they return to the realm of coexistence with the first-signal system and sufficiently accumulate the learning there, repeating the process of grasping the relationship between the first-signal system and the second-signal system, one day they will suddenly start talking with ease.

When they seem stuck with their words, adults should not bring them down by saying, "What's wrong?" or "What is it that you want?" Instead, they should say "Sure" or "I see," even if they do not understand. By listening to them carefully, the children will feel more relaxed and speak with confidence. Even while they talk about something they do not understand, they will gradually develop concepts in their mind. However, they cannot memorize the correspondence between these concepts of words and real objects and phenomena all at once.

Words corresponding to objects and phenomena that are familiar and repeated will likely be used correctly from a relatively early stage, but their specific usages will inevitably be learned at a later time. For example, children often drop the particles in sentences such as in "Baby sleep." or "Daddy work." This is because the concept of words has been completed and applied to visible, easy-to-understand things, but still not to the level of using proper particles.

In some cases, particles are repeated such as in "Go up up," or "Shoes off off," but this is also a phenomenon that occurs when the separation of the concept of the word is insufficient and the particle is not grasped properly. In this way, phrases that can instantly be recognized as incorrect can gradually be corrected, but with children, they often seem to understand when in reality, they do not have full comprehension.

According to an experiment by Soviet psychologist Sohin, when children are asked to put a small block on top of a large one they can do it well, but when requested to put a big block on top of a small block, it is said that mistakes will frequently be made. This obviously means that the Russian particle "on" was not understood as an independent word but rather in conjunction with the given circumstances.

Therefore, even if a child seems quite chatty and appears to understand, adults must continue to speak to them in various situations to help them learn the correct usage of words and their connections to objects. As they accumulate these experiences, children will become able to talk and think about things that are not right in front of their eyes but rather imagined. It will also become possible for them to play with a block while pretending it to be a train.

This can be done for the first time by clearly distinguishing between what is in front of them and what exists in their thoughts. This is the unique function of the second-signal system of words. Through this distinction, their thoughts expand from what is in front of them to their various past experiences, allowing them to make predictions about the future. Spatially, they will not be limited to where they are in any particular moment, and will be able to conjure distant words to mind.

As a rough guide for finding out whether this unique function of the second-signal system has been completed or not, we can observe the children's ability to successfully have conversations on the phone, or if they can play pretend—whether playing house or with trains—with verbal imitations.

When talking on the phone, they must grasp the meaning purely by listening to the words because they cannot see the other person's face or appearance. "Hello, this is Rocky. Have a good evening." It would be an issue if the conversation ended there. When asked, "Can I speak to your father?," it is necessary to be able to respond properly and say, "He's not home yet." Ideally, they would not just say what they want to say but also respond appropriately to the other person, and even strike up a conversation with them every now and again.

Even when playing pretend, they must not simply do what is commanded by the older children, but also exchange conversations appropriate to that occasion.

"Welcome, what are you looking for?"

"I want a carrot!"

"We don't have carrots today."

"Then please give me cabbage!"

In this way, it is important to be able to play the roles of customers and sales clerks.

Whether or not they can leave the realm of reality and think only with words is actually a crucial difference between animal thought and human thinking. Both dogs and dolphins are intelligent animals that can hear human speech and do various kinds of tricks, but many comprehend by distinguishing intonations and through visual analysis. They cannot leave the realm of reality and create new tricks on their own. It is a delay of this conceptual formation that is often seen among mildly autistic children and autistic children said to have improved through treatment.

In kindergartens and schools, there are some autistic children who can sit still at their desk, sing, dance, and even write *hiragana* and *kanji*, but have difficulty speaking coherently. They will respond to their name, but will not grasp colors or the concept of numbers. Compared to other children their age, their ability to think abstractly, apply new knowledge, and distinguish objects is lower. These children seem to be more developed compared to autistic children who do not respond at all and act indifferently. However, with further observation, it becomes clear that they have stumbled at the stage of conceptual formation and are having trouble moving ahead.

Typically speaking, children begin to say words at around one year old, gradually speaking longer sentences and increasing their vocabulary from around one-and-a-half years. The pace is rather slow. But when they reach the stage of conceptual formation at around two years old, they will rapidly begin to increase their number of learned words and speak longer phrases. However, in the case of mildly autistic children, this period of rapid lexical development does not arrive, and they will maintain the slow pace until about 3 years old.

Moreover, the content of their sentences remain in the realm of the fifth phase of the learning process of words mentioned earlier. Even if at 3 years old they point and say "I did it!" or "truck" while playing, or voice requests like "I want ice cream!," they cannot talk about anything other than what is right in front of them or what they want in that moment. Even if they come home crying, they won't be able to say, "Joe bullied me!" Even if they are frightened when told that their belly button will be taken away by the Thunder God if they don't cover it during a storm, they may retaliate by saying "No, no!" but not with snide remarks like "You're a liar!"

With these types of delay, even though parents become slightly worried, the people around them often assure them that "it's normal to see delay in boys" and that "they'll start talking in due time." They hear these words of comfort and feel relieved.

While thinking that they will start talking more soon, the child becomes two years old, and eventually three. It is around this time that parents begin to wonder if their child has too much of a delay. They worry and visit numerous counseling agencies here and there, and share that their children are experiencing issues with language development during their three-year checkup.

Many mothers say that their child "can't have longer conversations" or that they "only speak one word at a time." When I ask if the child can understand what is being said to them, half of the mothers say "yes" while the other half says "no."

From there, we talk to the children directly. In many cases, we discover that they cannot take correct actions with the instructions of words alone. We ask questions like "Can I have the building block?" without holding out our hands. We also ask about objects or people that are not in their field of view such as, "Where is the truck?," "Can you ride a tricycle?," "Where are your shoes?," and "Where is your mom?" Neurotypical children might make an annoyed face but point to the appropriate objects or people with their finger or chin nonetheless. But children showing a delay in language development remain apathetic, or simply do what they want to do without regard to what they are told.

In other words, even if the mothers believe they understand, it is often the case that they discern the meaning of phrases from the surrounding situation, and will become unable to reach comprehension by words alone.

When they are told, "Let's go shopping!," the child goes to the front door. But if the mother takes off her apron and picks up her shopping basket at the same time every day, the child will walk to the door whether they are told "Let's go shopping" or not. Just as people wave their hands when saying "bye" or bow their heads when saying "hello," words are often accompanied by actions. With interactions that are repeated almost daily, understanding them is easy.

However, neurotypical children usually reach this level of development at around one year old, so it would be concerning if a child has not reached this stage at three years old. Even if they are unable to talk on their own after the age of three, they would ideally be able to point correctly when asked "Where is your eye?," "Where is your mouth?," or "Where is your mama?" Furthermore, when asked "Can you ride a tricycle?," they might look around, find a tricycle, and go over to straddle it.

Some parents say that their children comprehend words when they feel like it, or that when they are absorbed in their favorite activities they do not listen. Others say they will listen to the mother but not the father. However, it cannot be said that children truly understand if their level of comprehension depends on the variables at hand.

Some children are shy and do not talk to strangers, but when left alone for thirty minutes, these children will often be seen staring at the other kids play or following them around. If they are forced into conversation, they might make a grimace and sit on a chair alone for twenty or thirty minutes. But as soon as their mother comes and says, "Alright, let's go home!," they cling to her arms and start talking. It is not until they are heard saying phrases like "I want ice cream!" that others realize they can talk.

As mentioned earlier, what is important in terms of language development is not "how much they can talk" but "how much they can understand." In particular, it is key that they can understand and act appropriately towards words that are not accompanied by a first signal. If a child has not arrived at this point by the age of three, they will not get to the stage of conceptual formation even at four or five years old.

Compared with children who do not talk or make eye contact, it is difficult to notice signs of delay in these children. But when the mothers are asked about the child's background and home situation, they tend to describe symptoms commonly seen among autistic children such as not crying as a baby, often getting lost, not crying even after getting lost and having to be taken home in a police car, and always playing alone.

Upon observing their growth henceforth, their language development will continue to be delayed as they struggle to sound out words in a precise manner, even after they turn four or five years old. Contrastingly, other children their age will usually begin making cheeky remarks, often to the dismay of their parents. They may not be able to distinguish colors or have developed the concept of numbers, handing three or four building blocks after being asked for two despite being able to count "one, two, three, four...." When shown some lines drawn on a page and asked to indicate the longest one, they might give an absurd answer like "blue." When asked to point out the differences between two pictures, they might say they are the "same." In this way, while they can interact on a superficial level, the concept of colors, lengths, and the differences between various objects are not yet grasped.

Seventh Stage: Thinking in Silence

When children become able to express the things around them—whether their shapes, colors, uses, and their own connections to them—using mostly words, share their personal experiences with others, and understand time and spatial concepts, it can be concluded that the earlier stage of conceptual formation has been completed. Of course, this means that they have learned basic operation methods such as word analysis and synthesis, and the content will become richer as they grow older. In this way, as comprehension and absorption of external matters progress, it will become possible for children to think actively with words and gain control of their desires and behaviors.

From the age of three, not only do children begin to express their desires and understand what other people say, responding and acting accordingly, they also begin to talk by themselves to no one in particular while playing alone. While stacking building blocks, they will say things like "Hi, Tokyo Tower! Very high, very high." Or when playing with dolls they might say, "If you eat so much, you'll get a stomachache! Bad girl." In these cases, the soliloquy of the child is a direct expression of their thoughts, and it can be understood well when seeing their behavior.

At this age, they think and talk simultaneously. So, when they are told to play quietly, they become confused. Their chatter in these cases is obviously not for the purpose of transmitting information, but simply for themselves. While it is true that even adults say their thoughts out loud when contemplating ideas, these children do it all the time. Therefore, it means that they will constantly be talking to themselves for a period of time.

In the past, this was known as "egocentric language" by Swiss psychologist Jean Piaget. According to his theory, this is caused by the fact that verbal acts are not fully socialized. However, as children grow and go through the socialization process, the egocentric language gradually disappears.

On the other hand, Soviet psychologist Lev Vygotsky said that egocentric language is in function a linguistic act that supports thought, branching out from the sociolinguistic act of communication. However, it was thought to be a unique form of "speech to self" that manifested during the child's transitional period which is not completely separated.

Therefore, with the progression of age, language is divided

into that which is used for communication and that which is used to think. Words aimed to facilitate thought ultimately become silent, internal language. A characteristic of internal language is that it not only becomes silent, but also changes qualitatively to possess its own grammatical and semantic structures. With this, the thinking process becomes abbreviated, condensed, and intuitive, inspiring ideas to instantly come to mind. Even in terms of behavior, people become able to take smooth actions without verbalizing their thoughts every time. The formation of internal language is said to take until three to seven years old, building up over the course of many years. It can be assumed that internal language has been formed when children stop talking to themselves and reading out loud.

Autistic children often stumble in the earlier stage of conceptual formation.

But these days, we are beginning to see so-called "unusual children" who are neither autistic nor neurotypical. For example, there are some children who have minimal issues holding everyday conversations but are quite restless and unable to sit still. They might say "red means stop" after being taught exactly that, but don't stop when approaching a red light. They might have no motivation whatsoever, do nothing but stand mindlessly in the middle of their classroom, or become silent at kindergarten or school despite being talkative at home. This is due to their inability to control their verbal behavior, indicating a struggle to form their internal language. This is the acquisition process of words as seen from conditioned response.

Although I did not directly touch on issues of intention and emotions nor the functions of our intellectual faculties, it is easy to infer from previous explanations that human beings cannot contemplate these problems without words. It can be understood that only with normal linguistic development are the healthy development of emotions and intelligence, as well as the ability to willfully control one's own behavior, made possible.

Chapter 3

Prevention First

From what I have mentioned up until now, I think it can be understood that autism is a much more serious disorder than is perceived by the general public, and it has a poor prognosis.

Even if TV is completely replaced by consistent verbal interactions as I have suggested, it is difficult for children who have passed a certain age to achieve normal development. If this is the case, our attention must be directed to what we can do to prevent autism in children.

In order to do this, I would now like to share some notes about childcare.

Talking is the Best Nutrition

When a baby is born, we give them milk. This is an obvious action that everyone takes. Parents pay close attention to whether or not their child's weight is increasing, concerning themselves about the amount of milk they drink each day. No one doubts that there is a causal relationship between drinking milk and weight gain.

However, it seems that the causal relationship of words are not so clear. Babies begin to laugh before parents know it. They will reach out upon hearing the word "hug," say "Mama" while chasing after their mother, and soon start saying phrases like "I want a book!" as though memorizing words were the most natural thing in the world.

Newborn babies do not understand human language at all, and they cannot learn words unless there are people who can teach them. To a baby who does not know anything, it might seem foolish at first to tell them how cute they are and ask what they want. But it is through these interactions that babies memorize words.

Of course, nobody goes up to a baby to discuss world affairs. Instead, they will typically talk about things concerning the baby, such as about their behavior and feelings. They might also share their own feelings to the child, or simply call their name.

By doing so, the baby captures the relationship between the first-signal system and the second-signal system. They gradually learn words and grow more like a typical human being. Direct dialogue from others will act as the milk for their language acquisition.

Without direct communication it is impossible to master words. In this sense, communication is like milk. But while a baby left without milk for three days will die, the consequences of absent communication are not as immediate.

It can take from six months to a year for a child to finally start responding to words or start saying simple words like "mama." In the meantime, it is necessary to consistently talk every day. Just from this one example, it can be observed that it is not easy nurturing a baby into an adult.

Don't Turn On the TV

From what I have mentioned so far, I think it is clear that direct communication is vital for a baby to learn words.

What can also be said from that is that television, radio, and other passive auditory activities are useless for language development. Not only are they useless, but in some cases they may slow down a child's response to the human voice and cause them to completely become unable to memorize words. So, when a baby is born, it is important not to turn on the TV and carry out childcare in this way. In fact, it is better to keep the TV off entirely until a child's first birthday.

Even after the first year, the speed of language development greatly differs among individuals. There are some children who utilize language as a second-signal system at about two years old, but many others will not be able to do so until they are past the age of three.

Therefore, in families with children under three years old, it is strongly recommended to turn the TV on as little as possible.

So, to what extent is it acceptable? This is a difficult question, but I think that the time to keep TV + radio + records on should be less than one hour a day. Although it may seem severe, I think it is inevitable to experience such inconvenience within the lifetime of struggles that children with autism and their parents will go through.

There are many ways to obtain knowledge such as by reading newspapers, books, and magazines, and entertainment can be sought in the occasional trip to a concert or cinema. To put it bluntly, everyone did this until about twenty years ago.

TV is Not a Babysitter

Certainly, there is nothing like television to give you the latest information, show the various sceneries of faraway worlds, and make you laugh and feel entertained all in the comfort of your own home.

Children love TV too, and if they start watching from around six-months-old, they watch it quietly. When they become one to two years old, they will look at the screen and dance, imitate, sing, and quickly memorize commercials. Due to this, adults tend to think that if they show their children television, they will absorb various information and become smarter. If a child sits in front of the television, they will not talk or cling to adults. In turn, adults will appreciate the quietude. Especially when preparing dinner, it becomes a struggle when a child comes into the kitchen and walks around. If they are frying tempura, parents might end up saying, "It's dangerous! Go over there and watch TV!" However, it should be obvious by now how greatly detrimental it is for children to be "babysat" by TV in this way, particularly from the perspective of language acquisition.

Often, children who were raised in a nursery or the like are said to have a late development of words. In these places, children do not experience enough verbal communication and life experiences so there is some delay. But by the age of four, they will be able to use words that allow them to communicate with the people around them.

For a while, it was believed that autism may be a form of hospitalism (institutional syndrome). However, there are only a few reported cases of autism in children raised in facilities. In addition, professionals of play therapy who aim to release the restrained minds of children through empathy and play, as well as those who place emphasis on mother-infant relationships (particularly physical contact, or "skinship"), tend to raise problems with the mothers' attitudes toward childcare during infancy. But none of the mothers I have met have particularly shown hostility or indifference toward their children.

Nonetheless, there have been many mothers who did not speak to their children enough, leaving the TV on without so much as a second thought. This was the result of their subconscious anxiety: "I thought it would be safe to show her TV. I kept it on so it could serve as a babysitter of sorts.," "My older child had no problem learning words, so I thought language development came naturally. I didn't proactively speak to my child.," "He was so quiet, I kept getting immersed in my knitting." I cannot help but think that even if they had been a little too absorbed in their knitting, their child would have developed well had they not been exposed to TV.

Even in cases I handle at public health centers, I rarely see case reports of autism among children from double-income families who had been brought up in nursery schools or by childcare workers from the age of zero. Some families of autistic children ran shops, but many were composed of businessmen and stay-at-home wives.

It is often said that babies are best brought up by their mother's hand, and women are often demanded to stay at home to tend to the family. With this in mind, it is an ironic phenomenon that autistic children are less common in families where the mothers work and seek the assistance of child-care professionals.

Here, we can compare how time is typically spent in the lives of a stay-at-home mom and a working mother. Stay-at-home moms spend longer hours at home, and in turn keep the TV on for longer hours as well. In June 1973 when I examined thirty-five households of children who came in for psychological counseling, I discovered that the time of television exposure was a maximum of sixteen hours a day, a minimum of four, and eight hours on average.

Even after asking various other people who I have met, it seems quite typical for homemakers to have the TV switched on for eight to ten hours a day (although not necessarily watching the entire time). In double-income households, TV exposure is usually around one hour in the morning at most. At night, it is around four to five hours. The difference in time spent in front of the TV appears to be key.

With a baby who does not yet talk, it is only possible to have one-way conversations. It is thought to be out of boredom and loneliness that the TV is then turned on. However, the baby is in a vital period of growth as it develops into an individual human being, so I urge all to turn off the TV and talk to them as much as possible.

TV Changed Our Lifestyles

As television entered households, the atmosphere, customs, and other facets of each family changed greatly. Among them, I believe it is the conversations in the home that changed the most.

In the past, everyone gathered around the dinner table and ate while talking about the events of the day. Now, most families eat while watching TV from the corner of their eye. Even if someone starts talking, the others are too focused on the TV and will only offer an empty response. There are families that turn off the television during meals, but it seems that they are few. During breakfast, the time is shown on the screen, so they eat while staring at the television instead of the clock. The news is on at lunchtime, so there are many families who keep the TV on for about an hour around noon. Dinner is the golden time of day when cartoons for children are broadcast.

I often meet parents during their child's three-year checkups who insist that "She doesn't settle down and eat.," or "He doesn't have much of an appetite." However, I think this is another effect of television. With the TV turned off, attention and direction can be given to the child, but with the TV on, both parents and children direct their attention towards the screen. This can make it difficult for children to focus on their meals, and they often try to finish eating as quickly as possible to go watch TV. After the meal, programs that the father and mother want to watch await. While mutual conversation was at least somewhat present during dinner, the topic of discussion is now centered around what is on TV.

Sometimes when I go back to the countryside or visit someone else's home, the hosts turn on the television for the evening news or other programs. The conversation dies down, and I start to wonder if I should stay or leave. On the other hand, the hosts simply turn the TV on as a force of habit, at times believing that it is also a form of hospitality.

At the age of two to three years old, children already have programs they want to see and they tenaciously assert their rights over the remote control. They remember surprisingly well which programs will be broadcast on what day, what time, and what channel. Even when they appear absorbed in a different activity, they will get angry if someone turns off the TV.

Around the age that they start elementary school, the time they spend glued to the television will increase. On average, they watch for about two to four hours a day. It is rare that they will spend less than one hour in front of the screen. Some kids will switch on the TV the moment they return from school. For them, a life without television is unimaginable.

When they go into middle and high school, many get their own television or radio and study with them on. While I admire their ability to focus with such distractions, I know they are often unable to feel comfortable in complete silence and end up keeping the sounds on until late at night. In this way, we are seeing the rise of a generation that "watches television from birth."

What kind of people will they grow up to be?

Discussing the influence of the content of TV programs is a complicated matter, and various arguments have been made. But in any case, once anyone is married and has kids, no matter how much they might miss it, I would like them to eliminate TV from their daily lives. In order to become able to do so, I would like everyone to pay more attention to how they incorporate television in their lives.

A baby developing autism because their parents habitually kept the television on would be an irreversible and regrettable consequence.

The Spread of TV and Autism

Mental disabilities and schizophrenia have been around for quite some time, but the emergence of literature and discussions about autism has been relatively recent.

The first documentation of autism was provided by Leo Kanner of the United States in 1943. Around the same time, Hans Asperger of Austria produced work about children with similar symptoms. In Japan, autism was first said to be recognized around 1952-53. However, it has only been over the past decade that autism has drawn the interests of many psychiatrists and psychologists.

I graduated from university in 1961 but I do not recall ever hearing about autism in lectures. I even asked other alumni before me, but no one else had heard it being mentioned in the classes as well. However, with alumni who graduated after 1965, it becomes clear that they had learned about autism in class.

With a new disorder like this, it is a fact that there is no accurate research regarding the prevalence of autistic children. But quite recently from June to July of 1974, a study was conducted by the Aiiku Research Institute targeting 575 autistic children over nine years of age who were part of the Parents' Association of Autistic Children. This was a study of children who were confirmed to be autistic. Detailed research was conducted on their current situation and educational status, although we will omit the results here for brevity. Instead, we will arrange the 575 children according to their date of birth. That is what you will see in the next figure.

Based on another study conducted by NHK, we can see that the trend is almost the same as the TV penetration rate of Japanese households. While the similar trends do not necessarily indicate direct cause, the epidemiological significance cannot be ignored in conjunction with the previous theory.

So, what about children with autism before the spread of television into the home?

As mentioned earlier, assuming that the main cause of autism is overstimulation of the auditory senses, radio sand records can also produce similar effects. Radios and records have existed before Kanner and Asperger's studies, so it is not strange to think that there have been autistic children since that time.

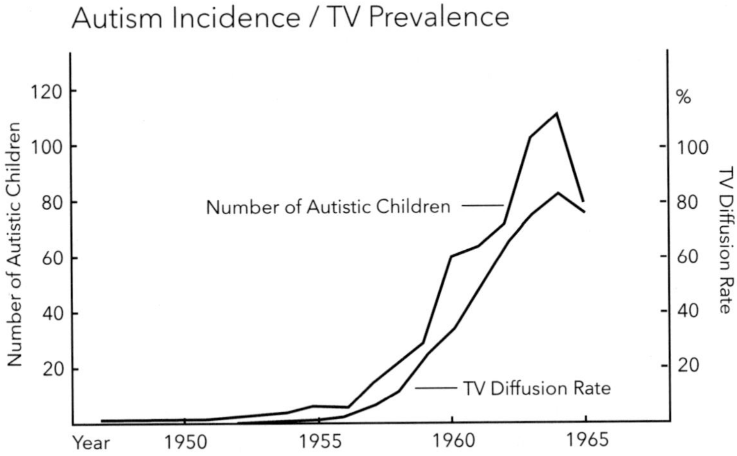

Kanner said in his first report that parents of these children were relatively well-educated and often economically blessed.

During his time, consumers of radios and records tended to be more affluent than most. Charles, a one-and-a-half-year-old who participated in Kanner's case, was already able to identify several symphonies at his young age, saying "Beethoven" after hearing the very beginning of the first movement. From this, it could be inferred that he spent a considerable number of hours listening to records at home.

Among the records of growth of autistic children, there have also been many cases where records were played during their early childhood. They knew many children's songs at one or two years old and sang well, even to the point that the parents considered having them study music because of their fondness towards music.

Parents tend to play records as a form of early learning. At first, children listen carefully, sing along, and try to guess the names of the artists. The parents will in turn work harder to keep the music going, repeating this vicious cycle. Before they realize, the parents discover that their children have not developed their language skills.

Yet, these points have not been touched on at all in past studies and reports. This is because they have not been thought to be in relation to autism, and they have fallen through the cracks when examining a child's history of growth. It seems necessary to reinvestigate whether radios and records were often played during infancy or from around one to two years of age.

Differences Between the Real World and TV

As mentioned in detail in previous sections regarding the process of language development, it takes a considerable amount of time for a baby to learn words.

Moreover, it is necessary for those around them to engage in direct dialogue appropriate to each situation during their crucial stage of development. As babies cry, laugh, play, and react in various other ways, it is important for others to create mutual exchanges by verbalizing their response.

However, images and sounds flow from the TV unilaterally regardless of the child's desires, behavior, or state. Whether the child is crying or sleeping, it does not matter. Of course, even if a child sees an object on-screen and tries to grab it, it is only an image and therefore cannot be touched. Additionally, even if they imitate what they see on television, no one around them will repeat it for them, praise them, or correct their mistakes. By the time a child responds to the TV, the TV will have already moved onto other content. In this way, television creates nothing but a one-way interaction from the screen to the audience. It does not take into consideration the state of its viewers.

So, it is only children over three who have solidly acquired language who are able to absorb new knowledge and words by watching television. For younger children, no matter how well they can imitate the TV or dance along to the programs, their voices and sounds are separate from their physical actions. In other words, it is not the true knowledge of the combined first-signal system and second-signal system.

In general, it is easy to think that a child will memorize some kind of information when they dance or express joy while watching TV. But as you can see in the language of autistic children, there is a possibility they will only memorize sounds and actions that are irrelevant to their day-to-day lives.

Also, since the TV is a machine, it will keep talking without ever getting tired.

In radio broadcasts of the Soviet Union, there are long moments of silence that make the listeners wonder whether their radio has broken down. But Japanese broadcasting technology is excellent, and no lull will last over two seconds. If the broadcast is interrupted for even five seconds, the hosts will offer a sincere apology. In this way, the programs run non-stop for eighteen to nineteen hours a day. This would be an impossible feat for a human being. No matter how talkative the person, they will get tired if they had to talk for three hours in succession. With piano practice, two or three hours is a good length to play. In any case, no human can continue to talk or keep their fingers moving for over ten hours a day without a break. However, this can be done on a TV or radio broadcast.

While there are surely no families that keep their devices on from the beginning to the end of the broadcasting time, there are families who switch them on the moment they wake up in the morning. They leave them on the rest of the day, and finally turn them off when they go to bed at night. This may not be detrimental to adults, but consider the babies who grow up being inundated by all that sound.

Unlike the radio, television comes with a screen. Children are lured towards the screen and end up sitting right in front of it. For this reason, they often tend to be exposed to this "flood of sound" for long periods of time, making it all the more dangerous.

Zero to one-year-old children do not fully understand the TV screen itself, but they often express pleasure while gazing at the images. This makes it appear as though they truly understand the content they are looking at. However, this can also be considered a type of orienting reflex mentioned earlier. In other words, the TV screen changes constantly.

This orienting reflex acts on the change itself, which is why the child is attracted to the TV screen. There are not many things around children that change so rapidly without any effort on the part of the child. Even if they don't hold out their hands or get on their feet and walk, it will show them something new.

So, is not it that children are being drawn to this novel sensation and looking at the screen forever? Also, in the same way as sounds, the TV screen does not look the same to children as it does to adults. The real world is three-dimensional, but the TV screen is two-dimensional.

According to one experimental study, it is not until the age of three to six years old that children will be able to see two-dimensional images on a flat plane as three-dimensional images with depth and perspective.

Babies will begin to crawl and move on their own from about eight months after birth. At this stage in their development their hand-eye coordination also improve, and they will start grasping depth perception in the world around them.

However, this is within the range of very familiar living situations that they can move around in. It will take years to look at the television screen and be able to interpret it from a three-dimensional perspective. In addition, the television screen produces images—not real objects.

The images are not stationary, but are constantly moving. The images appear to move because they follow the same principle as movies: stroboscopic movement. Stroboscopic movement is a phenomenon in which light appears to move from one point to another when two lights are illuminated consecutively at very short intervals. If they are illuminated more than twenty-four times per second, the awkwardness diminishes and the motion will appear fluid. NHK TV currently broadcasts at a rate of thirty frames per second. In other words, the screen changes thirty times per second. Stroboscopic movement can appear differently according to age. The lower the age of an individual, the more stroboscopic movement occurs at longer time intervals.

According to one experiment, in six-year-old children there is already spurious exercise at 1048 sigma (1 sigma is a thousandth of a second), whereas for adults it is 160 sigma, about one-sixths. For example, when light first flashes at point A and then at point B, as the interval at which this light flashes is shortened, it appears that the light moves from point A to point B. In the case of adults, light does not appear to move from point A to point B unless the interval of the lights is less than 160 sigma. If it is a longer time interval, it will look like point A and point B are shining separately.

The experiment described above was conducted on all ages up to thirteen years old, but according to the study, the older the individual, the shorter the time interval required to see immobile points as mobile objects.

Since the experiment is difficult, no experiments were conducted with children from two to three years old. However, it is easy to guess that the stroboscopic movement will occur with longer time intervals as the age gets younger. So even when viewing the same screen, images appear different for children and adults. In addition, television is shown via scan lines that run quickly, unlike movies that utilize films for each frame. On NHK television, the number of this scan line is 525. That is, it is calculated that 15,750 scan lines run in one second.

When children learn to walk, there are also situations in which they come running into the room when the TV is turned off to switch it back on, regardless that they were not even watching it from the other room.

The parents say, "They don't seem to be listening, but are they?" I think this is also a kind of orienting reflex.

When the sound of the TV is interrupted, it means that a change has occurred in the environment, and orienting reflex may occur in this case.

This is similar to a person living in a noisy place—usually in the vicinity of a motorway or a railroad— staying in an inn on a quiet mountain, unable to sleep because of the silence. For them, the state of having background noise has become their norm.

I think this is the same as the so-called *nagara-zoku* ("tribe of multitaskers") that cannot study or relax unless they put on the radio or a record. However, since this "tribe of multitaskers" has already acquired language, this does not lead to delayed language development. Trouble arises when these individuals get married, have kids, and continue this multitasking state.

I believe that children should be brought up in as quiet an environment as possible after they are born.

The Dangers of Radio

Since television has become prevalent in households, there is a view that the radio has been pushed aside. But in reality, it continues to play unnoticeably for long hours every day. This can be observed most often in shops.

In barbershops, for example, they play the radio as a means to service their customers or to get better business. Some leave the radio on out of sheer boredom as they receive fewer customers during the day.

This would not be an issue if there were no babies or children, but I have seen butchers listening to the radio while looking after their child, or babies sleeping in a small room in the corner of a vegetable store with the TV on right beside them. Such scenes concern me. When I encounter them, I can't help but meddle in their business by thinking, "I wonder if there is any way to put them in a nursery as soon as possible?," or "It would be better to turn off the radio…"

The second most common is the car radio. Driving for long hours—especially on a highway—can be a monotonous and at times sleep-inducing activity. So as not to cause an accident, many drivers listen to the radio for stimulation. But, they often have a child in the vehicle. Even if it's not a big deal to drive with them occasionally, I often see children in delivery cars being taken along on deliveries with their parents. Children love cars and driving with them is not an issue in itself, but I would like the parents to turn the car radio off.

Sightseeing buses also often play the radio as a show of hospitality. I have had experiences where even though I was tired and wanted to sleep, the sound of the radio was too loud and distracting for me to rest. Sometimes I wish they would ask the opinions of the passengers before unilaterally turning on the radio.

Even at small to medium-sized factories, here are places where the radio is played as background music. If it is just for adults that would be fine, but if it is a family-owned factory, sometimes there are children and babies on the premises.

Either way, I would like everyone to make sure that there are no young children under the age of three before turning the radio on for long hours at a time. Although this may seem overly sensitive, I believe that we must give at least this much attention in order to protect our children.

The Dangers of Records

Japan is one of the world's leading producers of light electrical appliances, and likely has one of the world's top penetration rate of radios, stereos, and tape recorders, not to mention television.

In recent times, even among families living in small, one-room apartments, it has become commonplace to have a television, radio, record player, and tape recorder (including cassettes) in the household. The sales of records and cassette tapes are also increasing in correspondence.

In the past, record players were typically only seen at dance studios and public facilities such as schools. Now, however, they are found in every home alongside high-quality stereo equipment. Some families even have two record players for the parents and children to use independently.

To take full advantage of this, record companies have also released various types of records for children. In the past, they released nursery rhyme records at most that contained only three-minutes of song. Nowadays, there are LP records for children that are thirty minutes long. These contain not only nursery rhymes but stories, read-along books, music for infants, and much more.

There are even subscription services that send a new record and book every month. It is advertised that if children listen to such fine music from a very young age, they grow to become children with rich emotions, quick language development, and intelligent minds. However, is this truly the case?

In the same way as television, I think that for infants younger than three, it is inadvisable to play them records for the same reasons mentioned above.

No matter how breathtaking the performance or how well a narrator talks, once it is packed in a record, it turns into unilaterally flowing sounds that cannot be changed according to the condition of the baby.

A lullaby is soothing because the mother sings while gently rubbing the baby's back. No matter how off-key her song may be, no record can take her place. Even when it comes to reading books to a child, a mother is an amateur. She cannot read out the scenes like an actor. Still, it is good to pick up a book and read with children while watching their expression. If a child says, "That's a crab!," the mother can respond with "Yes, that's a crab!" This kind of communication is not possible with records. If the parents put a record on, the child will be glad and surely ask them to play it again. Some babies even stop crying the moment their mother puts on a record.

However, even if the child is satisfied on the spot, it does not mean that they will grow up well. For babies, what matters are words. Without words, no matter how musically talented they may be, they cannot become a musician. No matter how much money is spent on high-quality stereos, nursery rhymes and classical music, and stories read by famous actors, none of this guarantees the healthy development of a baby.

Beware of Sound-Producing Toys

There are many kinds of toys, but children delight in playing with toys that make sounds. Rattles, *daruma* dolls that clatter as they roll around, whistles, and drums have been long beloved by kids.

*(Note: The Japanese **Daruma** doll is a hollow, round, modeled after Bodhidharma,*

the founder of the Zen tradition of Buddhism.)

Dolls that used to make only one sound when placed on their back can now say a plethora of phrases with a pull of a string. These toys are soundless unless children or adults use their hands to produce noises, and the sounds usually stop once the toys are put down.

However, there are now battery-operated toys which have become popular since the war. There are trains and cars, hopping rabbits, and drumming bears. In the past these were all wind-up toys, but today they all run on batteries.

Children are pleased because the toys never cease to move, and parents buy them because there is no need to keep winding the springs. However, imagine now noisy it will get when the toys are switched on for a whole hour. (So, in most households, the toys end up abandoned once they break or their batteries run out.)

Whatever the case, once they are turned on, these electrical toys will not stop moving until someone stops them. All the while they move, they make very loud sounds. In some cases, I believe these sounds may create an obstacle in the acquisition of words.

Another toy that has caught my attention are the *kusudama* balls that are attached to music boxes for babies. While they used to be wound by hand or triggered by a spring, these days they run on batteries.

(Note: The Japanese ***kusudama*** is a paper model that is usually (although not always) created by sewing multiple identical pyramidal units (usually stylized

flowers folded from square paper) together through their points to form a spherical shape.)

Babies will certainly be delighted and will remain quiet while the music plays, but if they are kept on for a long time, I think it will have the same effect as the sound of the TV.

When I told some people my hypothesis that autism is caused by television, a few of them went around to ask parents about their children's exposure to TV and radio during infancy. One of them told me that they had met an autistic child, but they did not grow up with TV, radio, or records.

What other than TV, radio, records, and tape recorders make sounds?

I kept on thinking.

Then one day, I went to a friend's house and found the sound-producing *kusudama* ball. When her baby became upset, she pulled the string of the music box. We talked for a while after that, but noticing something noisy, I looked around to see the *kusudama* ball spinning around. I thought it was distracting, but because I was a guest at another person's house, I could not go and stop it. Then, I realized that the music box would continue to play for all eternity.

I was amazed by the fact that such toys even existed. But since babies are not able to stop them on their own, I would like to suggest that they are turned off after being played for a short amount of time.

Language Cannot be Acquired Later

After the settlement of the thalidomide lawsuit in Japan in October 1974, the issue came to a close. However, it is not possible to create the hands and ears that the children were not able to develop at a later time. They have to carry this burden on their backs for the rest of their lives.

Similarly, in the case of children with autism, language that could not be acquired is impossible to learn once they grow older. The process of development cannot be restored.

Just as the hands and ears that were not formed in the fetal period cannot be grown after childbirth, the words that could not be acquired in infancy cannot be learned once children are old enough to attend school.

There are quite a few individual differences in learning language, but no matter how late their development, children must be able to communicate with other people by the age of four. Once they are older, it is already too late.

Turning the TV Off

Recently, various types of pollution have been raised as issues. With regard to sound, the noise of airplanes, bullet trains, and automobiles is a problem. These sounds give a feeling of discomfort that cannot be easily endured, but it is not as though they can be completely removed from our lives.

There have also been an increase in local residents' movements urging the management of the sources of these sounds. It is not enough to wish noise pollution away. To alleviate it, efforts must be made to negotiate and fight for the cause.

However, in contrast to such noise, the sounds of television, radio, and music flowing from records are pleasant to adults. Indeed, they are produced willingly with a flip of a switch. Conversely, this means that they can be eliminated just as easily.

Contamination of air and water is hard to see at a glance, but in the case of sound, it is clear. When TV and radio are switched off, silence comes back. Apart from noise coming in from the outside, these sounds in the house will not be present unless they are intentionally switched on.

If you agree even just a little with my hypothesis, I would like for families with small children to carefully consider the aforementioned arguments in order to prevent the development of autism. Let us not turn the TV or radio on in households with children under three years old so as not to regret it later.

Chapter 4

How to Identify Autistic Children

In the previous chapter I described normal language development and the symptoms of autism, but in this section, I will share what to look out for in children who are thought to have a delay in language development.

For children exhibiting steady growth, the expectations regarding their level of comprehension at one year old or what words they should typically know at two years old can be found in most childcare books, so I would suggest using those texts as reference.

Delayed language development can be divided into three categories: "Delay of simple words," "Intellectual disability," and "Autism."

Even after the age of two, children with a "delay of simple words" often have a limited range of vocabulary, are unable to pronounce words clearly, and have difficulty understanding what people they are not used to communicating with are saying. Despite being able to say individual words such as "out" or "want," they have trouble connecting them into phrases like "Go out." or "Want cake." Mothers become extremely worried when this continues even after they reach two-and-a-half or three years old.

However, if the progress of their physical development and potty training is smooth, and they can eat on their own and play well with other children, there is not much to worry about. Even if they are unable to respond verbally to both parents and strangers, if they can respond with appropriate physical actions there is little that merits concern. These children may show delay in the words that they produce, but since they understand the words spoken by those around them, they will catch up to the speed of average development by the age of three-and-a-half to four.

"Intellectual disability" can be characterized by late development as a whole from infancy, and in general, both the height and weight of the child are less than average. Even when they reach the age of three, they still need their diapers in the daytime, cannot eat on their own, often spill their food, and are unable to use chopsticks well. The age they take their first steps is also late at around two years old. Their general movement is slow, and even when they are spoken to or played with, their reaction is hazy. They often watch other kids play but do not actively try to join them. They are sometimes left out or even bullied.

Compared to the children with a "delay of simple words," they speak fewer words and can only say simple words like "mama," "me," and "want" at around the age of three. They will respond to their own name, but when spoken to they will show little more than a blank expression.

In this way, the fact that they show a mild reaction is what differentiates them from autistic children. Though slowly, these children will gradually increase their range of vocabulary so long as they are talked to, offered various experiences, placed in group settings, and given verbal stimulation. When they reach school age, they will be able to have conversations with little to no inconvenience.

Contrasted with these children, autistic children appear quite different. First of all, when they are less than one year old, most mothers describe them as "not needing much attention," "not laughing even when played with," or "not shy." Some mention that they do not make eye contact. All in all, they exhibit very little reaction from infancy, and seem to have no interest in their mother. Some have little interest in milk and food, while others eat as much as they are given. Sleeping a lot is another symptom. They sleep well day and night. Many mothers say that if they let them drink milk, they sleep well and do not cry. They describe them as angelic, easygoing babies.

Thus, autistic babies have various symptoms, but what is used as an important indicator common to all children is that they are not shy around strangers. Other characteristics such as not making eye contact or not laughing during play somewhat depends on each child, but not being shy around strangers is common to all autistic babies. It is also difficult to improve. Shyness is a phenomenon that does not appear unless a clear visual perception of the family's face has been established, so I believe it is one of the first indicators of intellectual functioning.

In terms of physical development, as with neurotypical children, their weight and height increase at an average pace, and they typically take their first steps at around the same time as most other kids. Around the age of one and a half years, the majority of children begin to walk steadily and learn to speak several words.

When they start walking, it will be hard to keep track of them while they run around stepping on objects and pulling things out of every drawer they can find. With neurotypical children, if they are scolded a couple of times or get hurt, they will not repeat the same mistakes again. With autistic children on the other hand, they will be unfazed no matter how many times they are scolded. They will move around a lot but with no uniformity in their actions. They will climb up to high places, walk in the middle of the road, and go every which way in an unpredictable manner if their parent releases their hand. They are highly active, but can barely perceive the situations they are in. Even if they get lost, they will rarely cry. Even when their frenzied mother finally finds them, they do not express joy or any particular emotion.

They also show strong tendencies during playtime. Instead of playing with dolls or building blocks like many other children, they would rather turn a toy car upside down and spin its wheels, run water from the faucet and watch it flow, or arrange whatever they see in a straight row. Even if they are introduced to other children, they are mostly indifferent and continue to play on their own.

There are many children who like television and records very much. Sometimes they keep them on all day long and make a big fuss when someone turns them off. It is not as though they are watching TV quietly, however. In fact, many of them move around and around, coming back to the screen only when they hear their favorite commercial. When that's over, they go off to do something else. But when the parents think they are no longer watching and turn it off, they run back to switch it back on themselves. Even with records, a child will remember their favorite one. Despite being unable to read the words, they will learn to distinguish their favorite record and go as far as to play it without the help of anyone else.

Though they will see an overall delay in their language development, it is rare that they will not be able to speak at all. Proper conversations will be difficult, but they will voice requests, repeat words, or talk to themselves. Still, their way of speech will be quite different from other neurotypical children.

The most important characteristic is that they will be unresponsive and indifferent to the words of others, almost as though they do not hear them at all. Even when their name is called, they will not turn around.

With autistic children, they are often seen as "strange" rather than "behind." While neurotypical children change and progress little by little every day, autistic children show little progress from one to two years old. Moreover, their unusual behavior persists.

The onset of autism is usually between one and two years old, but in some cases, they develop normally until around the age of two or three and suddenly stop singing. Or, when asked "Do you have to go potty?," they will offer nonsensical answers like "The beer was delicious!" It is not until then that parents begin to find it strange.

These are some of the ways in which to distinguish autistic children. If you think that your child applies to the previous points, please refer to the following chapter to regain their development.

Chapter 5

From a Therapeutic Point of View

Up until now, I have spoken mainly from a preventive point of view, but I would now like to concretely describe what you should do in the case that your child seems to have autistic tendencies and delayed language.

Completely Turning Off the TV

I think that the dangers of keeping the TV on for a long time have been demonstrated in the explanation so far, but it is very difficult in the present era to banish the television completely from home.

For preventative measures, I think that it is okay to pick what you want to see, such as news and dramas, for one or two hours a day. But from a therapeutic sense, TV should be completely eliminated for it to be effective. Many people think that when they have a TV, they talk less to their children, which is why it would be better to turn off the TV and increase communication. However, this is not the point I am trying to make.

Autistic children tend to show little response when spoken to, making it seem as if their hearing is bad. Even if it seems that they have no issues with their hearing, their level of responsiveness fluctuates, and there are times when they can hear and when they cannot.

I think that the lack of response to outside communication is due to the fact that they have not gained the orienting reflex to the voice which is the first stage of language acquisition. Because these children have been exposed to the sound of television for a long time the human voice has completely lost its novelty, and even if they are spoken to, the words do not conjure any feeling of surprise. So as the first step, they must feel an unfamiliarity towards voices, a surprised reaction of "What is that?" To do that, it is necessary to eliminate the TV completely at all costs.

Of course, the same goes for radios, records, and cassette tapes. You must get rid of all items that produce artificial sounds and create a quiet environment. Some parents decide to play records when turning off the TV doesn't work, or play it for a few hours out of guilt for cutting out their child's favorite programs. However, this negates all of their efforts. What they need is quiet.

In many households, the TV is off during the day but turned on in the evenings for the older children. I am asked sometimes if it is OK after the children have gone to sleep because TV is the only source of nighttime entertainment for their father. I understand the lingering attachment to television, but do not turn it on whatever the case. Using earphones is OK.

If the older children want to watch TV, please convince them to keep it off for the future of their brother or sister. I have heard that even a four-year-old cooperated when his mother said "Your sister will turn into a fool." However, if there is a program that they would like to see by all means, you can explain the situation to your neighbors and let them go watch at their house during that time. There are many people who worry that without television, their children will go to school or kindergarten and have no common topic to talk about with their friends, leading them to be left out of the group. But in actual cases, children will find many other topics to talk about. After all, television is not all that exists in a child's world.

The next problem is the father. First, please tell them the reason why they have to eliminate TV. If they understand that it is for their cute child, they will surely agree to it. If they don't want to experience the decades of hardships of raising children with intellectual disabilities, it will be unavoidable to give up their own pleasures for a couple of years.

Adult can go to the movies, read newspapers and magazines, and find plenty of other entertainment and news sources besides television. In the case of fathers, they are often convinced easily at first, but in the first or second month when some changes have started to appear in the child, they will start turning the TV on again because "We've kept the TV off long enough," or "There's just one sumo match I'd like to watch," or "There's a night game on tonight," and so on. Unlike with children, mothers cannot demand the fathers to turn off the TV. Since the fathers have the most authority in the family, their opinions must be respected to a certain extent. For this reason, the mothers often end up giving into their wishes.

However, when the TV is turned back on in this way, the children's language development stops at the time when it was first eliminated. Once neurotypical children begin to babble, they will gradually increase their vocabulary and speak longer phrases. But with autistic children, if the TV is turned on when they start speaking baby words, their language will not develop from that point on.

Certainly, the number of learned words increases little by little, but they will not be able to talk about things that are not in front of them, nor understand colors and the concept of numbers. Even if they can talk properly on their own, when spoken to by other people they will not try to listen at all, say nonsensical words, repeat words, or otherwise fail to show normal developmental progress.

Therefore, I would like families to turn off the TV not only until their children learn to speak words and conduct daily conversations, but until it is believed that they have understood the concept of words as mentioned in the previous chapter.

As parents tend to have a biased view of their children, I want them to listen to the opinions of the nursery school, kindergarten teachers, neighbors, and the rest of their community. Only when they feel that their children are at more or less the same level as other kids should they consider turning the TV back on.

No TV for Two to Three Years

So, how long should you turn off the TV? I think it is best to eliminate TV for at least two to three years. Although it is not easy to believe that there is developmental delay in such children because of their average body growth and facial features, their language development is equivalent to that of a zero- or one-year old child. Thus, they are extremely behind. To make up for their delay, it will take two to three years at best.

In the cases we have seen, parents are shocked at first and turn off the television. Still, once they see the slightest change in their children, many think that "they are OK" and turn it back on. The power of TV is impressive.

After about a month with the TV off, children will begin to turn around when they hear their name and start to speak words. However, this is very low level as it is the stage when orienting reflexes have finally manifested towards words.

If you turn off the TV for about three to six months, parroting will be reduced, everyday conversations will be smoother, and comprehension will improve to the point where they could stay at home alone. They will learn to keep the house clean and settle down overall. From the parent's perspective, this will seem like a massive improvement from the previous state. However, this is still the level of one-year-old neurotypical children, and there is still delay.

Neurotypical children will continue their smooth development, but even if autistic children improve to a certain level, they will remain at that stage if the TV is turned back on at that time. For the child, it is great progress to become able to answer and greet people, or point to the correct body part when asked "Where is your eye?" After all, they did not speak at all previously. Their vocabulary will also increase little by little.

However, this is the language linked to the first-signal system of actual scenes, objects, and requests, but not the higher-level use of words as a concept. It would take even a neurotypical child two years to reach this stage, so it would take more time for autistic children. With that in mind, it is important not to feel happy with small changes and to train with a consistent policy.

Just by eliminating TV for about three to six months when they are three years old, mildly autistic children will reach a point of having no inconveniences in daily conversations and thriving in collective life at kindergartens and schools.

Yet, looking at these children at the age of five, we notice that their phrases are short compared to other children, and they do not enthusiastically start conversations. They cannot grasp the concept of numbers over two or three, and cannot make sense of analogies such as "If sugar is sweet, then what is salt?" They may be unable to distinguish between elephants and lions, and they do not have sufficient ability to think and discern with words.

In kindergarten life, there are a lot of learning and activities accompanied by the first-signal system such as songs, plays, and arts and crafts. If children progress enough to make simple everyday conversation, they can manage to keep up with the others. Without the ability to operate concepts via language, however, there seems to be considerable hindrance to learning from around third grade.

If you are a parent, you probably want to put your kids in an ordinary class. Additionally, as there are many schools now that admit all prospective students, the levels of special education classes are very low. If one wishes, children with a slight delay can join the regular classes. If the teacher is understanding, even severely autistic children can be included.

After that, however, children diagnosed as autistic are usually transferred to the special education class, or must switch to a special needs school from elementary or junior high school. It is said that only about one in 100 autistic children can go out into society as fully independent adults.

As you can see, the prognosis for autism is very bad. No matter how much these children study from elementary or junior high school, their efforts will not bear fruit. Completely eliminating television at the young age of three to four years old will decisively affect subsequent development.

Next, I will introduce actual cases in which children changed after completely turning off the TV from the age of 3.

Case S

Born in May 1971. Has a brother two years younger. Male.

July 1974: Three-year checkup and psychotherapy counseling
(Three years and one month)

[Main concerns]

- Delayed language development.
- Excessive crying.

[Mother's account]

He will start to cry immediately if the route home is changed or if things don't go his way. He started talking after the age of two-and-a-half, but I do not know if he understands what other people say to him. He does not answer to questions like "Do you want to eat X?" or "Do you like Y?" He does not say "papa" or "mama" on his own.

He is apathetic towards food and will not eat until given food.

He likes cars and stares at them from the window, but he does not play with the other children.

When he was an infant, he was very quiet and I did not have to give him much attention. I don't remember him babbling.

He does not watch specific TV programs, but he likes commercials and songs. He memorizes them quickly and repeats them.

[Behavioral observation]

- While reading picture books he might say "Uhh" or "Ahh, bus." But other than that, he only repeats what he hears on television.
- He cannot communicate linguistically, but he has had

contact with other children and psychologists.

- He also laughs when he sees his brother (one year old).

(The psychologist at that time was different, and she had not advised them to turn off the TV.)

August 1974 *(Three years and two months)*

[Mother's account]
When I asked "Are you cold?," he repeated, "Are you cold?" This is not a conversation. When I ask "Where's daddy?," he answers "Daddy work," but it seems to be only because I taught him so.

Although he does not respond to questions, he can clearly express requests such as "Want juice," "Want milk," or "Bread!"

We live on the fifth floor of a 2DK apartment. He does not go out alone.

The mother does not speak much and the father is also silent. He only interacts with the children for about half a day during the entire week.

His father is absorbed in television on Sundays, and there is hardly any conversation at home. We have color TV and have it on from around 7:45 to 10:30 AM and from around 6:00 to 11:00 PM. Even when he was younger, TV time was almost the same.

We sometimes play records but never the radio.

[Behavioral observation]

- We have a picture book of a car. When I ask "What's this?," he repeats "What's this?" However, he can read the Roman alphabet correctly such as in "NHK," and can correctly identify things he points to like "truck" or "airplane."
- While reading "Testing of Words" (written by Taguchi Tsuneo and Sasanuma Sumiko, published by Nippon Cultural Science Co., Ltd.), when I ask "What is swimming in the water?," he answers "Fish" many times. However, he can't do the same for other questions. He points to tricycles when asked "Which is the pencil?" With pictures, he can identify a few such as "apples."
- When I hold him, he sits quietly on my knee. When I say, "Can you sing Agnes Chan's song?" he does not respond.
- He makes eye contact. He is attached to the mother. He has a small body but he moves a lot and has an average facial structure.

[Guidance]

- Turn off all TV.
- Talk to him as much as possible.
- Take him outside.

September 1974 *(Three years and three months)*

[Mother's account]

When I switch off the TV, he does not care to watch it at all and does not try to turn it on by himself. So, only after he's asleep at night, we sometimes watch TV for about two hours (he can't hear it).

He has starting talking on his own. It started with single words, but he's now forming sentences like "Baby read book." When I ask "Are you cold?," he replies, "Not cold." Recently, he has started saying "I'm not cold." However, there are also many times when he simply repeats words.

He keeps close to me and cries "Mommy!" when he falls. Before, he was calm even when his toy was taken away, but now he makes a big fuss whenever other kids so much as touch his toys.

[Behavioral observation]
He sometimes answers correctly such as when I asked, "What did you ride on?," and he answered, "I rode the bus." But he also often repeats words. For example, when I asked "What is the baby's name?," he could only say, "Name ...?" However, when I asked "Which ones are your shoes?," he pointed to them correctly.

October 1974 *(Three years and four months)*

[Mother's account]
There weren't any big changes as in the previous month, but he does not repeat words as much. Before, he would immediately repeat the same words he heard, but now he cocks his head as

if saying he does not know.

He has forgotten most of the popular songs he knew before, and he no longer sings them.

November 1974 *(Three years and five months)*

[Mother's account]

We never turn on the TV.

He has learned how to say phrases appropriate to each situation such as "Ryo (younger brother) sleep.," "Eat soon.," and "Take bath."

[Behavioral observation]

- When the psychologist asked somewhat difficult questions such as "Does Ryo also get sad?," he goes back to parroting words.
- Simple things in front of him seem to be well understood.

December 1974 *(Three years and six months)*

[Mother 's account]

He rarely repeats words anymore.

Previously, although he was able to stay at home alone, now he always wants to go out with his mother.

He cannot dress himself well yet.

[Behavioral observation]

- At the consultation room, he likes the duck toy and has been pulling it around all the time. When asked "It is fun?," he answered "It's fun.," instead of repeating the question. However, when asked "Where's the duck's head?," he pointed to the mouth. To the question "Where's the duck's leg?," he pointed to the tail.
- When his mother told him they were leaving, he cried and said, "No! I don't want to!"
- When his mother picks up the younger child he asks, "Mommy, only you go on bus?" Detailed matters are difficult, but he has become able to respond.

[Guidance]

- At this time, I was asked by his mother, "If the sound of the television is bad, how about tropical fish tank heaters? The thrumming sound is quite noisy, especially as nighttime." She also inquired, "We will go back to the countryside during New Year's, but they will probably have the television on over there. Should we not go?"
- To these I answered, "Aquarium heaters should be turned off if possible.," and, "The TV may be on during New Year's, but since the people around him will talk and play with him, it's better to take him along."

January 1975 *(Three years and seven months)*

[Mother's account]

New Year's Day, we went to the countryside with my husband for three days.

We played a lot there.

When asked "Who did you play with?" after coming back from outside, he was able to answer, "I played with Seiko." When asked "What did you do?," he answered "Swings and slides." I also asked, "Where did you park your bicycle?," and he pointed to a general area. The bike was eventually found, so he has become able to talk about things that are not right in front of him.

[Behavioral observation]

- When I show the book "Testing of Words," he proactively points and says "Fish," or "Bow-wow (cat)." However, he cannot answer questions such as "What flies in the sky?" or "What swims in the water?"
- As to the question "Which is the pencil?," although he previously pointed to the tricycle, he was able to correctly answer four out of five questions.
- He memorized most of the picture words, but he sometimes mixes up watermelons and apples, elephants and cats, rabbits and cats, leaves and apples, and so forth. Thus, he cannot distinguish different objects clearly.

March 1975 *(Three years and nine months)*

[Mother's account]
He seems to understand, but he does not truly understand. He only knows what he can see.

He has good athletic ability, but is clumsy when wearing and removing clothes.

He once caught a cold and could not go out for two weeks, and he has not wanted to go out since.

[Behavioral observation]

- When I show him a stuffed dog, he smiles and embraces it.
- "Where are the dog's eyes?" — He points correctly.
- "Where are your eyes?" — He points correctly.
- "What do you do with your eyes?"— He tilts his head.
- "Where are the dog's ears?" — He points correctly.
- "Where are your ears?" — He points correctly.
- "What do your ears do?" — He remains silent.
- "Where is your mouth?" — He opens his mouth and points to it.
- "What does your mouth do?" — He opens his mouth, put his fingers in, and says "Food."
- "Where is the dog's tail?" — He points to the feet.
- "Who did you come with today?" — He answers, "Bus."
- He can express his requests and what is in front of him quite well, but functional and abstract expressions are still insufficient.

April 1975 *(Three years and ten months)*

[Mother's account]

Yesterday, he joined a weekly outdoor nursery for the first time, and he did the same activities as the other children. He also managed to play and when I had a discussion away from him, he joined the other children. He sat still during the picture-story show and sang songs with everyone.

In terms of his lifestyle, he has become able to pull his pants down and go to the bathroom, button his pajamas, and use keys to open locks by himself.

He often remembers patterns and signs that he sees.

He has begun talking to others frequently from himself.

[Behavioral observation]

- When asked "What is this?," he answers correctly as in, "This is a handkerchief, I wipe my hands with it." However, when shown a picture book with an injured child with a bandage and asked "What happened to this girl?," he answered, "She is playing with her mother." Thus, he does not catch the details.

[Findings]

- Simple conversations can be held, but he does not reply to abstract ideas.
- The conceptual formation of words is still insufficient.

May 1975 *(Three years and eleven months)*

[Mother's account]

He speaks but does not understand abstract concepts, which is frustrating.

When he plays with other children, he seems to fit in because they do not talk abstractly.

At the outdoor nursery, he cried when he bumped into another child. He did not cry before.

He sometimes replies "Here!" when the teacher calls the name of another child. When the other children laughed and his mother scolded him, he resisted and did not speak after that.

His father comes back home only once a week. His father seemed to think that his child would get better right away, so he seems somewhat frustrated.

[Behavioral observation]

- He plays by putting wooden blocks and many other toys into a basket.
- "What is this? (Dish)" — "It's for tea."
- "What is this? (Cup)" "Drink."
- "Is there a cup of you?" — "There is."
- "What color?" — "Cup color."
- "What kind of toys do you have at home?" — "There are toys."
- "Do you have this (stuffed doll)?" — "No."
- "Are there building blocks?" — "There are."
- "What else are there besides building blocks?" — "Look,

over there..." (He shifts the conversation to other topics.)

[Findings]

- Abstraction by words is still insufficient.
- It will take another six months to a year...

June 1975 *(Four years)*

[Mother's account]

Recently he wanted to go shopping by himself, so I sent him off to buy *yakitori.* He succeeded.

When I asked him to go buy milk, he was able to do that as well. In other areas, there is not much progress.

He understands aspects of everyday life, but when it comes to more complicated things, he replies but says only what he wants to say. For example, when he is asked "Is your father at home?," he says "Yes," even if he is not.

At home, I wonder why he is unable to understand such simple things and get angry. But upon reflection, I know I should have more detailed conversations with him.

At the outdoor nursery, he watched a movie for an hour and reported what he saw to his dad.

In the past, he could not distinguish between "buy" and "get," but now, when he gets something, he shows it to me first.

[Behavioral observation]

- While making tunnels with building blocks and playing with Legos (a toy with wheels on the blocks), he says "This is a train, and so is this one, and this one, too."
- When shown two identical Lego wheels and asked, "Are these the same?," he says, "Different."
- He often goes to his mother saying "Water" or "Sweaty..."

[Guidance]

- In the coming year, he will focus on acquiring the abstract abilities of words.
- Adults should talk to him proactively with phrases such as "You can eat rice and side dishes.," or "Bear, building blocks, doll—these are all toys."
- To expose him to interactions with other people, sending him out to buy things is encouraged as much as possible.

July 1975 *(Four years and one month)*

[Mother's account]

He cannot understand simple commands like "turn around" and "pull down."

There are times when he has difficulty distinguishing details and shakes his head from side to side. "It's here," he'll say, but when I ask "What's here?," he'll simply repeat "It's here." without clarifying the "what."

I worry that he will not be able to go to school like this.

But when he is asked "Who did you play with today?," he can answer "xx-chan and xx-chan." When asked "What did you do?," he can say "We threw stones." or "We went to the park."

He stirs up his brother two years younger by saying things like, "Go hit mom!"

His younger brother talks more, but he is violent to him.

[Behavioral observation]

- He often plays with his brother.
- He pushes and pulls the chassis on his Lego cars saying, "This goes on here.," or "These came off." He happily pulls cans with magnets on them saying "Here it comes!"
- When he asks "Where is the water?" I tell him, "Over there!" He repeats, "Over there?," and tries to walk away barefoot. When I say, "What about your shoes?," he comes back and looks for his shoes.

[Findings]

- A year has passed since I started to consult, and he has made progress in his conversations and behavior. Nobody can tell what is wrong at first glance.
- He also interacts with other children.

September 1975 *(Four years and three months)*

[Mother's account]

He has finally started to understand the words "up" and "down."

After I taught him the word "opposite" such as when he put his shoes on wrong left and right, he did not make the same mistake afterwards. However, when other people ask him, "Do you have any siblings?," he has a hard time answering.

He can also say phrases like "It's starting to rain." and "It's dark so dad will come home." However, it is still impossible for him to distinguish temporal concepts such as "yesterday" and "today." and sometimes he replies randomly without clearly understanding what other people say.

[Behavioral observation]

- "The psychologist who you met here before, is she here today?"
- "She's here." (She is not)
- "Do you know that psychologist?"
- "Yes." (In fact, the psychologist was there for the first time)
- In "Testing of Words," his comprehension according to purpose was three out of five, and instructions by name he was able to answer all eight correctly.
- With picture words he had wrong answers, such as calling a rabbit "cat," a cicada an "insect," and a monkey a "horse." "How do rabbits jump?" "They don't jump." "How does a cicada scream?" "They don't scream."

November 1975 *(Four years and five months)*

[Mother's account]

We decided on a two-year kindergarten nearby.

He had no trouble in his everyday life, and he could understand things if I told him.

He now understands "brother," "up and down," "front and back," and "right and left."

He plays outside from morning till evening until it gets dark.

There have been no particular incidents in which he has been picked on or has not been able to keep up with other children.

The television was turned off at home for one year and three months, but he watches when he goes to other people's houses.

Because other kids watch cartoons and such, I would like him to watch too, but what is the recommendation?

As a mother, since other children watch TV, I am worried he cannot find mutual topics to talk about.

[Behavioral observation]

- Here, he plays with his brother well.
- Conversation is also lively.
- In "Testing of Words," he has made many mistakes with nouns such as calling rabbits "cats" and rats "dogs."
- Seeing a picture reel with an overturned boat, children

throwing a rope and pulling it up, and finally turning the boat back over, he was able to explain only that "the boat is turned over and the children are standing up," and could not understand that they were helping the boat.

[Guidance]

- In terms of conversation and behavior, he is almost no different from neurotypical children, but still lacks the ability to capture abstract meanings and causal relationships.
- If he goes to kindergarten, I think he will make a lot of progress there. However, I would still suggest not watching TV for two years until next August. Even if you decide to only watch cartoons, when you put it on, you will end up watching TV for long durations.

May 1976 *(Five years old)*

[Mother's account]

He has entered kindergarten from April and is happily going there.

It seems that he remembered a couple of friends' names.

He often plays with his friends and seems to understand the teacher's instructions.

Recently, he became interested in letters and is now able to read his own name.

He seems to watch TV when he goes to the neighbor's

house.

Perhaps because he does not watch TV, he likes picture books.

He understands how to use money, so I give him thirty yen and send him shopping.

He is getting better overall but I think he still lacks focus.

[Behavioral observation]

- Today, his brother did not come.
  "Why is your brother not here today?"
- It seems that he did not understand the meaning of the question well, and he names a few of his friends.
  "Is he at home?"
  "He is at home!"
  "Who is with him? Dad?"
  "With dad."
- His mother explained, "Your brother is Ryo. He got hurt, so we took him to stay at ××'s house."

[Findings]

- Although he has become able to speak well, there are still times when he provides random answers to questions he does not understand well.
- He's almost there.

November 1976 *(Five years and five months)*

[Mother's account]

His teacher said that he was growing steadily during a personal interview at the kindergarten.

His drawings hung up in the classroom are not great, but they are not outstandingly bad.

His drawings of the school's sports day showed a flag, but he only used one color.

He does not use other colors unless the teacher tells him to do so.

He makes promises with friends at kindergarten and plays with them after coming home.

If he does not understand and I say, "You are stupid.," he cries and says, "I hate you! Go away!"

During conversations with adults outside the family he still tends to match his opinions to theirs, but that is not the case when he is with friends.

He can share what happened at kindergarten that day and tell me "I have a letter today from school."

He has become able to write his name.

He knows numbers from one to ten.

[Behavioral observation]

- He is playing with a toy with his brother.
- "What did you do today at kindergarten?"
  "I made a string phone."
  "How do you make a string phone?"
  "Crumple the paper, paste here, and put the string on."

"Could you hear with the string phone?"
"I could hear."
"When can you not hear?"
"When the string droops."

[Findings]

- He became more active compared to half a year ago.
- He is moving his body while instructing his little brother a variety of things.
- He can accurately explain the order of steps when making string phones, and he can grasp the causal relationships of things.
- He has come another step further.
- There should be no problems from here on out.

January 1977 *(Five years and seven months)*
Home visit

[Mother's account]
When he first started kindergarten, even when he said that "the teacher told us to bring a box," I could not trust him and would call a friend to check.

Nowadays, I've become able to feel secure about what he says.

When he comes back from kindergarten, he plays outside until around 4 o'clock.

I asked his kindergarten teachers, but they said there is

nothing troubling going on there.

I now let him watch TV about thirty minutes to one hour a day.

When it's time to watch TV, I turn it on.

When it's time to turn it off, he turns it off by himself.

He does not watch TV for long periods of time.

[Behavioral observation]

- He is playing in his room with his brother. They play games and do projects found in magazines.
- He brought out trains he already made, disconnected two of them, and pulled a string saying, "This is how you move them."
- "Who made this?"
  "Dad."
  "It is as nice as I expected."
  "Look, this part spins."
- He comes out with a cut-out, "How do you cut this?"
  "Cut here! (between the feet)"
  "No, it'll fall apart if I cut it here."
- Pronunciation and intonation are normal.
- He does not repeat words he hears and responds quickly to what he understands.
- Took an intelligence test. Intelligence index: 106. Average.
- He is somewhat petite, but he is quite expressive and active.

[Findings]

- He has reached average level of intelligence.
- Even at kindergarten, he does well in groups with the other children and his expressions are the same as neurotypical children.
- With this, we conclude his examinations.

Symptoms After Turning Off the TV

Some children show no response when the television they have become used to watching is turned off. However, there are some cases where the child with cry as soon as it is turned off, and unable to tolerate the intensity of their cries, the parents turn on the television again.

There are children who cry quietly, while there are others who seem as though they have suddenly developed dementia. Parents become worried, and in some cases, they play records under the assumption that they are at least better than TV.

In the case of drug addiction, abruptly ceasing to take the drugs will trigger withdrawal symptoms. But the series of reactions described here may also be said to be a kind of withdrawal symptom of television addiction.

Even if the withdrawal symptoms are quite intense, they will ease in about a week. No matter how sorry you may feel during this time, do not turn on the TV or play records. If you compromise here, you cannot expect any further progress. If you overcome this, you will see progress little by little, but not necessarily in a straight line.

Usually about a month after turning off the TV, children will begin to turn around when called, sit down to eat, and generally head in a good direction. But it is often the case that after a couple of months, they will not leave their mother's side or will start crying during meals, becoming more difficult to handle. In the case of these children, it is easy to think that this phenomenon is troublesome especially because they showed little interest in the mother and rarely cried before the television was turned off. Actually, it shows mental progress.

So, after a couple more months, they will better distinguish words so that when their parents say "Please wait.," they can stay at home alone for a while and eat by themselves. Depending on the child, some will trouble their parents after about six months by saying "No" or "Stupid!" to everything. But as a whole, their vocabulary will increase and their facial expressions will become enriched, so parents should be pleased by such a phenomenon.

Also, after turning off the TV for a while, as though they have developed a TV phobia, they might cover their ears and make a strained face when the television is on. They will respond similarly to the sound of the speakers of sweet potato trucks, and when they are shown TV at kindergarten, they will cry so much that they are forced to sit outside. In such cases, the TV should be turned off if it can be, but since it is a temporary phenomenon, it is not necessary to worry excessively. It is better to wait until the time comes that they become accustomed to these sounds.

Anyway, do not worry about small changes. We need to firmly keep track of how the children are changing in units of one or two years.

Eliminating TV Long-term

From a therapeutic standpoint, if you do not completely cut out the TV long-term, it is difficult to hope for the normal development of the child. However, nowadays it is very difficult to completely eliminate television for long periods of time.

Even if it can be kept off for three to six months, there are many cases where children go back to the habit of watching television to watch "just this program...."

Among the fifty cases I guided in the past three years, it was only one or two households other than S's that completely eliminated television for more than a year.

To eliminate television for a long period of time, there is no way other than selling it or giving it to another person. My conclusion after three years of guiding families to "turn off the TV" is that the only way to succeed is to not have a television at home.

I want you to throw away the television completely for the sake of the children.

Taking Away Their Favorite Things

Neurotypical children also like mini-cars and sleeping with stuffed animals, but when other children come to play, they will play together and respond to their conversations. However, when autistic children are given toy cars, they will spend an entire day rearranging and playing with them. Even with calendars, rulers, or watches, they just look at the numbers and show no response towards the outside world. It is characteristic of them to only show interest in one specific thing. Traditionally, it has been said that it is good to give children whatever they show interest in and to draw out the talent of the child from there.

However, when they are keen on these specific things, they do not respond at all to their surroundings. This was why one mother proposed we take away objects of the children's interests. I asked them to do it if they could. I had several households hide their children's favorite picture books, building blocks, and toy cars.

When they did so, there were some children who remained calm and others who cried violently. Some children pretended everything from an abacus to a box was a car, while others pulled out their mother's cookbooks in place of their favorite picture books. In this way, there were various children including those whose interests moved from one thing to the next.

As a result, even if they cry or make a fuss, it is better that the children begin to focus their attention towards their parents as they will increase their vocabulary and become interested in other things. But depending on the child, they will pull out objects in the house one after the next or, upon having their toy cars taken away, run outside to the parking lot to look at cars instead.

So now, I ask families to hide what the children particularly like as much as possible, but if they cannot keep order in the house, leave some of their favorite toys out and wait until they become less fixated on those objects. When used in conjunction with other methods, they will calm down as a whole, increase their vocabulary, and no longer be so obsessed with certain objects as much as before.

Snack Restrictions, Food Restrictions

For the past four years I've been focusing on teaching "completely cutting out TV," but unfortunately there are still several children who have not calmed down nor increased their vocabulary even after six months to a year. Even after cutting out television like other households, I cocked my head in bafflement at why those children were not getting better.

Then, in June 1977, I met three-year-old "S." She looked overweight when I first saw her, so I weighed her. She was twenty kilograms. (Same weight as the average six-year-old child) I said to her mother, "She is overweight." Her mother replied, "Yes, she usually eats a lot of rice. Because we also have lots of drinks for our restaurant (Chinese restaurant), she drinks five or six bottles of Ramune soda or juice a day." Being much too heavy for the age of three, I instructed the parents not to give her any kind of juice. Even if she cries, they must not open the stopper.

When she came back a month later, she had stopped crying as much as she used to. When her mother said, "Has daddy been good?," " she patted her father's head. When told to clean up, she put toys into a box one by one. Even though she hardly spoke before, she was able to wave her hands while saying "Bye-bye" and refuse while saying "No!" When I weighed her, she had lost one kilogram and was nineteen kilograms. She was no longer sweating profusely.

However, after a month she came back again, but she did not show any improvements compared to the previous month. Her weight still remained at nineteen kilograms. When I asked about the situation at home, her mother said that once she stopped letting her drink juice, she began eating a lot of rice during meals, as much as two bowls of rice from an average-sized bowl. It is natural that her weight did not decrease.

I found out that good results cannot be achieved even if the TV is eliminated, as long as the child ends up eating too much.

Looking back on the cases without much progress from this perspective, I noticed children like "D" who was sixteen kilograms at the age of two years and five months but put on three kilograms in eight months, leaving him at nineteen kilograms at three years and one month, or "T" who weighed fifteen kilograms at the age of two years and two months but weighed two kilograms more seven months later, putting him at seventeen kilograms at two years and nine months.

When I observe the other children who come to see me, while they may not be overweight, there are so many who are the same height and weight as children two to three years older than them: "H" who is 104 centimeters tall and weighs eighteen kilograms at three years and ten months (looks five to six years old), "A" who is 112 centimeters tall and weighs twenty-three kilograms at four years and ten months (looks six to seven years old), and "E" who is 125 centimeters tall and weighs twenty-seven kilograms at five years and eleven months (soon to start primary school but looks like a third grader). These children are so big that I think for a moment that the wrong child has entered the room.

So, I decided to ask what kind of foods they eat. I discovered that many of them drank a lot of milk as babies and eagerly ate their baby food, gaining weight at an unusually fast pace from ten kilograms (weight of an average one-year-old) at six months after birth to fourteen kilograms (weight of an average three-year-old) at one year old.

When I asked them their favorite food, I heard the same answers such as curry rice, hamburger, spaghetti, ramen, and udon. When asked how much they eat, even two and three-year-old children said they ate adult portions of curry rice and ramen and two servings of hamburgers. In addition, if they like eggs they will eat three or four at once, and if they like fried shrimp they can devour ten or more. While portions varied for each child, there were many cases where the children could eat their favorite foods limitlessly, and happy parents encouraged them to do so.

When I asked what they dislike, I was repeatedly told "raw vegetables and fruits."

Neurotypical children similarly like curry rice and hamburgers, but they also eat vegetables and fruits to stay nutritiously balanced. However, neurodivergent children absolutely refuse to eat foods they do not like.

No matter how small they are cut up, if such foods are picked up and put in their mouth, they will spit them out. They also consume a lot of milk. Some children drink 700 to 1,000 cc of milk every day. It seems that parents think it is okay for their child to drink large amounts of milk as it is a "perfect source of nutrition."

Also, among children who do not eat vegetables, there were cases in which juice was given to compensate for this. Every day, they were given 1,000 cc of 100% fruit juice purchased from the supermarket.

Some of the children who drank close to 1,000 cc of milk and fruit juice exhibited below-average height and weight. Because they would be full from all the liquids they consumed, they could not eat much else.

Also, there are sweets. They could easily finish two pieces of cake, an entire 100-yen chocolate bar, and large bags of snacks such as potato chips. They like snacks very much. They do not have set snack times and are given what they want when they want it. The snacks are bought without fail or else they will grab them without permission. When going outside, the mother will put a lot of sweets in her bag to prevent them from making a big scene and embarrassing her, because they are quiet as long as they are eating.

Certainly, if they are neurotypical children they will be able to understand, but neurodivergent children would not understand what their mother says. Giving food is the fastest way for parents to get them to follow instructions or stay quiet.

As a wisdom of life, it is easy to understand that parents are trying to maintain a semblance of normalcy by giving food to keep them quiet, but it would be a problem if this results in the worsening of their condition. Therefore, I decided to measure the height and weight of the children who came in for a consultation every time. I soon noticed that the children who do not improve gain weight at an abnormal pace, such as two to two-and-a-half kilograms in six months. In comparison, the children who do improve do not gain much weight.

Babies gain roughly six kilograms in a year, but usually the rate of this increase slows down after their first year. On average, babies gain two to two-and-a-half kilograms a year from the age of one to three, and around one-and-a-half to two kilograms a year from the age of three to six. It is abnormal for their weight to increase by three to four kilograms per year.

I concluded that these children are given too much to eat, and that giving a lot of food in this way is causing a type of excessive stimulation and, as a result, the deterioration of their condition.

Ordinarily, what you eat enters the stomach, is digested and absorbed, and the rest is excreted as stool, so it is only the internal organs that work when you eat food. It is often believed that the brain has no part in this process. But the secretion of saliva and gastric juice and the feeling of needing to go to the bathroom or feeling of hunger are carried out by the work of the brain. Therefore, eating will give various stimuli to the brain.

Even in Pavlov's famous experiments of dog saliva and conditioned reflex, the observation is that the stimulation of food enters the brain and the saliva necessary for digestion is secreted when a dog is given a piece of meat. Therefore, I believe that giving too much food causes excessive stimulation to the brain and makes its normal function out of order.

So, I tried implementing the restriction of snacks and other foods as one of the cure methods. After trying various methods, the most successful way has been what I will describe below:

First of all, as a rule, no snacks are given in the morning. In the afternoon, a very small amount is given at around three o'clock (one to two rice crackers, a handful of snacks, or mandarin oranges just enough for them to quickly eat up).

When taking them grocery shopping, firmly refuse to buy snacks even if they grab them off of shelves or cause a ruckus. Wait for thirty minutes or even one hour until they give up and stop crying. If this is done for about a week, they will eventually give up and stop making a fuss.

Milk should be limited to about 200 cc and should not be kept in the house. The only drinks they should have are water or barley tea instead of juice or probiotic drinks.

As for meals, try not to make dishes that children like to eat such as curry rice, spaghetti, and hamburgers. This is because they will eat their favorite foods endlessly.

Additionally, in the case of children whose height and weight are greatly above average, all side dishes including rice and bread should be reduced to half of the usual amount they have been given. Neurotypical children will say "No more" if they have eaten enough, and will not eat even if they are given more. But with neurodivergent children, the brain function that automatically stops them from overeating does not work properly. If there is food in front of them, they will continue eating as much as possible. This is why we must forcefully limit their food intake.

But while I suggest such restrictions on snacks and food, it is much more difficult to actually put them to action. Some mothers falter at the difficulty, saying that it is "much harder than turning off the TV" or that it is "heartbreaking to see them cry."

When restrictions are placed on their diet, children open the refrigerator, the cabinets, lick butter, lick ketchup, lick sugar, and try to eat anything seemingly edible from flour to toothpaste. They seek food and put whatever they find in their mouth, and the only way to combat this is to keep the fridge and cupboards empty. Parents or siblings should also stay on alert as their food might be snatched from the side.

Even if the mother lets the child eat, when the father comes home and sits down for dinner, the child will often want to eat again. But if the mother gives in and feeds them more food, the treatment will have no effect. It is imperative to keep food completely out of their sight and allow them to eat only the amount they are served at any given time.

It is hard enough to turn off the TV, but when parents have to restrict their children's diet on top of that, it will be so difficult at first that both parents and children may shed tears. But these tears will last only for about a month. After two or three months later, the children themselves will stop eating so much so quickly, and parents will start to get the hang of the treatment. More than anything, the children will start to talk and look attentively at their mother's face, leaving the parents with hope that their child will improve. Their unbalanced diet that worried the parents so much will be gone as though it had never been a problem at all.

However, in some children, various symptoms appear temporarily like the withdrawal symptoms when cutting television. There are many cases in which they cry profusely. They might be quiet for about an hour after a meal, but will cry for two or three hours after that. Once they have finished crying, they might then show slower movements, sit all day, roll around on the floor, stop responding to the words of others, and have a blank look in their eyes. There are times when they will be unable to say words they have previously been able to say. It is also characteristic of them to sleep for very long hours. It is just like an adult in a depressed state.

Most mothers are shocked to see this, but as this condition continues for about a month, the children will begin to move again little by little. They will start pointing, talking, and understanding what is said to them. If it continues longer than a month, it is recommended to increase the portion of their meals little by little. What is important during this stage is to remain quiet without not talking to them excessively or taking them out.

When they are sleeping, do not force them to get up. This is because the brain temporarily stops responding to outside stimuli, and during this time the brain takes a rest. The various pathological symptoms are alleviated, and once they get well, the children will naturally restart their activities.

Also, it may happen that they do not pass stool or urine. If their stool comes out about every other day there is not a problem, but when it does not come out for more than three days, the portion of their meals should be slightly increased. For urine, they should be given a lot of liquids and water-rich fruits like watermelons if they go less than three times a day.

In the cold season from autumn to winter, these dietary restrictions are not problematic, but as the temperature rises and the metabolism of the body becomes more prosperous, children develop light dehydration symptoms. So, during the hotter seasons from May to September, there should also be a decrease in meal restrictions.

Dehydration symptoms include a sudden high fever, white chapped lips, constipation for over three days, urination less than twice a day, and diarrhea lasting more than two days. If they exhibit any of these dehydration symptoms, it is suggested to visit a hospital for IV drips or shots to alleviate them.

In order to prevent such symptoms, let them drink water and barley tea as much as they like. They can also be fed vegetables and fruits multiple times during meals, so when they do not want to drink water, they can be given more food. In this way, we proceed while keeping in close touch with the families.

Thus, temporarily, we reduce the amount of food considerably, reduce the weight of the child by one to one-and-a-half kilograms, wait for their symptoms to settle, and then increase the portion of their meals little by little as they get better.

However, increasing the portion of their meals has to be done carefully. Even with the slightest increase, the child may go back to their original weight and simultaneously back to their lethargic state. Eating one cake too many may even cause vomiting or diarrhea. Therefore, instructions on when to decrease or increase food intake vary for each individual child depending on their current state.

What I felt after offering dietary counseling is that the parents also eat very well. If I say, “What a big child!,” many parents say, “We’re big too, so it must be hereditary.” But upon further observation, it becomes clear that big people also eat a lot. If you ask what they eat and try to calculate their calorie intake, you will find that they eat between one-and-a-half to two times the necessary amount. Since they monitor the amount of food their children eat from that perspective, even if a child eats two big hamburgers in one sitting, they do not get the impression that it is too much.

In addition, though we had not instructed snack and food restrictions for small children and children who do not like to eat at home, after about half a year of counseling, I have found that large children who have followed a strict dietary regimen have shown greater improvement. So, I once asked the smaller, less voracious eaters what they eat in a day. It was then I discovered that they nibble on ice cream and candies and drink probiotic beverages. I instructed them to quit snacking altogether. Then, they improved their unbalanced diet and began to eat a variety of foods. Their height and weight increased, and at the same time, they became responsive to the words of those around them. They also began showing interest in their surroundings and got better overall.

Turn Off the Night Light

Recently, there has been an uptick in home visit consultations and I sometimes stay overnight at a patient's house.

In December 1977 when I stayed at one particular house, I woke up in the middle of the night to see light seeping in from a crack between a pair of sliding doors. Since I am usually unable to sleep unless the room is pitch-dark, I thought it rather strange for a moment. The next morning when I asked about it the mother answered, "Yeah, I've been keeping a light on all through the night. I've been doing it since the baby was born. In the middle of the night, it's hard to turn on the light each time I need to get up to give milk or change their diapers."

So, after I came back, I started asking patients if they kept a light on at night. It turned out that quite a lot of them did. There were only three families who said they do not leave a light on. Some of the families decided to turn the light on at night, despite not doing so previously, after eliminating television from their home. As their children cried and did not sleep unless a light was kept on, they resorted to doing so during the night as a result. Once this continued for about half a year, some children finally became able to sleep with only a mini light bulb on. However, there were others who would wake up in the middle of the night, and upon realizing that the room was completely dark, begin to cry hard. So, when I told families to turn off the lights completely, I found that some children began to cry awfully. This is why now, I instruct them to turn off the light after the child has fallen asleep.

However, if the baby wakes up in the middle of the night and cries, turning the light on may cause them to wake up and play for one or two hours. For this reason, it is best not to switch on the light. After a couple of days, the baby will stop waking up in the middle of the night. Because the brain also rests during sleep, it is better to be exposed to as little stimulation as possible.

Although it is not recognized by our consciousness, even if you are sleeping with eyes closed, the light will still come into the brain.

Try comparing the brightness of the room when you close your eyes and when you cover your closed eyes with your hands. Even with closed eyelids, you can see how bright or dark it is. Even during naps, you can sleep better if you dim the room with thick curtains and lie in the dark. Also, in the summer, since it becomes bright outside from around 4 o'clock in the morning, it is ideal to keep the room dark until it is time to get up by closing the shutters or investing in thick curtains. Layering dark, ordinary curtains will also make the room quite dark, but if possible, use blackout curtains used at movie theaters to make it pitch-black. You can buy them at curtain stores and home furnishing shops.

Speak Normally and Do Not Go Out Often

Up to now, I have said "turn off the TV and talk to the children," but some of the mothers say that they have tried to speak from morning till night until their voice has faded, or, regardless of what the child is looking at, say,

"That's a bakery."

"The signal is red."

"There is a fish store over there.," in a unilateral manner.

The mother's feelings are painfully understandable, but this also makes them tired and is not effective. It is true that their language acquisition is delayed, but unlike neurotypical children, autistic children exhibit a slow response to speech itself.

When you turn off the TV or restrict their meals, the variety of pathological symptoms such as lack of eye contact and disappearing the moment you let go of their hand will alleviate, and they will start to look at your face when you talk to them.

In this way, if you talk to a child after they have become fully receptive, they will remember more and more. In the same as a baby learning words, this will not be achieved in a mere two to three months. It will take one year, possibly two. So, do not rush, and just like when talking to anyone else, talk to them in your day-to-day life. It is enough to simply say "good morning" when we wake up in the morning, or "Time to eat!" after preparing a meal. There are people who forcibly say "Hello" or "Goodbye" until their communication is reciprocated, but this is too much. It's good enough for parents to say a greeting once or twice, bow, shake hands, and show them how to interact with others. In half a year, they will be able to do the same.

There are also cases where the parents will call their child's name over and over again out of joy of receiving a response, only to find that their excessiveness pushes them to stop reacting. Some others make them say "A - I - U - E - O (Japanese vowels)," try to teach them "Give me!" gestures, or do not give them what they ask for unless they say "Want." However, this also brings about negative effects. If you force them too much, they may become able to do these actions, but as a whole their comprehension will not improve and the number of learned words will not increase.

Also, it is not good to go out too much. I once examined a three-year-old child who was restless and taciturn despite not being exposed to the television for three months. When I asked about their living conditions, I was told, "Before we turned off the TV, she used to watch all day long. When we turned it off, she started wanting to go out more. There was a time where we would chase her around outside all day long except when we sat down for meals." When I advised this child not to go out as much as possible, she became quite calm in three months.

Whatever the case, for two to three months from the start of therapy, I advise parents to limit the time spent outside to about two to three hours until their children start to settle down. While monitoring the state of the child, I gradually loosen this restriction.

When going out to places where there are other children such as parks, children are often given sweets and snacks. When out shopping, there are times when children will cry in want of a treat, and the parents will give in "just this once." However, whether it is candy, ice cream, or juice, do not give them anything even when outside. No matter how much they cry or roll around on the sidewalk, if you project the attitude that you will not buy them anything, they will stop begging after the second or third time.

Long distance driving is also bad. Autistic children tend to like cars very much, and they'll have no trouble sitting in a car even for five or six hours. Some children stop crying immediately when sat inside a car.

In recent years, there are more families with cars, and it is not unusual for cars to be their main means of transportation. Although you do not feel much when you ride a car, the engine is quite noisy and the car radio is often turned on out of boredom. There is little to do but look outside, and we do not move our body at all. It does not add to our experiences and our legs become weak.

Even though they were potty trained, there was a child who stopped expressing their need to go to the bathroom after about five hours of driving. There was also a case where a child, after coming in for an examination from Shikoku to Tokyo on the plane, had a screaming problem for about half a month.

There is little to be nervous about if pathological symptoms disappear, the child becomes calmer, and their vocabulary increases rapidly. But if they have just started to show signs of calmness, the smallest occurrences can trigger a relapse. It is best to refrain from going out or taking them for long drives until about three months after they have started to settle down.

Does Excessive Stimulation Cause Autism?

In this way, we are currently trying various treatment methods, but there are children who do not get much better even after six months to a year, and still others who show smooth improvements.

Originally, I thought that autism was a mere developmental disorder of language. I believed that progress would be made as long as the children's linguistic comprehension improved and they began talking, and I made this my main goal.

However, if you carefully observe children who learned to speak in one or two months, you will see that before they began to talk, they learned to turn around when their name was called, had lively eyes and looked at others properly, and did not go off by themselves even when no one was holding their hand. On the other hand, children who struggle to show progress often do not turn around when called, and if they like something, they become extremely attached and will try to find alternatives to that object when it is taken away. They are often restless and cannot go out alone with confidence.

So, I have found that rather than desperately trying to teach them words through speech, it is faster to try and eliminate their unique behavioral issues until they are able to respond appropriately when spoken to. Also, with autistic children, they do not only exhibit unique responses during communication, but they are also either abnormally sensitive or insensitive to sound, images, touch, taste, and smells.

What usually first stands out to parents is when their children do not turn around even if they call their name. Many mothers think their child has hearing loss and visit an ear, nose, and throat doctor, but find no abnormalities upon examining their ears. When a specific television commercial begins they would come flying into the room, so it seems that it is not an issue of the ear itself. When I examine such children, although they do not respond to normal voices, they might come running after hearing the small rustle of a bag of snacks. In this way, while they might generally be insensitive to sound stimulation as a whole, they will react sensitively to specific sounds.

Even in terms of vision, while they may not be able to distinguish their parent's faces from the faces of strangers, they will seek out particular logos or anything that interests them no matter how small. The eyes of autistic children are also generally different from other children. They tend to lack vigor and are slightly off focus, not looking towards anyone who talks to them. Still, when those children are immersed in their favorite activities or causing mischief, their eyes will suddenly gleam with excitement. When in sunny places, they will form wrinkles on their forehead and narrow their eyes, reacting very strongly to the brightness of the sun.

In terms of touch, they like nylon stockings and will eagerly touch anyone's feet. Or, on the contrary, if even the slightest bit of water or food touches their skin, they will make a big fuss and will become obsessed with keeping clean. Some children loathe being touched, and even refuse to be held by their own mother. Others do not like to wear socks even in winter, taking them off the moment they are put on. In the summer, some children lie around in the shade or on the cold concrete floor, or prefer to be naked.

Autistic children also tend to have extremely unbalanced diets. They might only eat rice crackers and peanuts, absolutely refuse to eat vegetables, or be exceedingly picky about their food. If forced to eat, they will spit the food right back out. This is because their sense of taste is very sensitive, but on the contrary, some children can easily drink spicy kimchi brine or beer that neurotypical children will spit out in an instant.

In terms of olfaction, there are kids who sniff out the pudding of specific manufacturers and eat them exclusively, or smell whatever they can get their hands on. This is because their sense of smell is extraordinarily sensitive, and they can smell things that most people cannot.

While there are abnormalities with these senses, there are no abnormalities in their sense organs such as eyes, ears, and tongue. Rather, it seems that there is an abnormality in the sensory center of the cerebrum which is responsible for the sense organs.

Although this is not a sensation, there are also abnormalities in terms of sleeping. Some children, despite reaching one to two years old, sleep abnormally well all night and day. On the other hand, there are those who do not sleep well, cry, or wake up in the middle of the night and play for one or two hours. In the morning when it gets a little brighter, there are children that get up at four or five o'clock and cause some parents to struggle.

Even in terms of athletic ability, while there are children who can disassemble miniature cars instantly with their bare hands, there are three and four-year-old's who cannot throw balls, make origami, or use scissors. They may be clumsy with their hands and while they walk, and overall are inferior in terms of athletic ability.

Thus, in autistic children, not only behavioral aspects but also sensory aspects show various anomalies. Even children who have learned to speak exhibit these behavioral and sensory abnormalities. There are cases where these abnormalities remain until later on in life, and being unable to keep up the same pace as other children, they struggle to assimilate into group life.

Also, even with children who have learned to speak, there is a lot of talking to oneself and parroting words. They might be able to express demands and repeat commercials but unable to have a conversation, mimic the right intonations, and otherwise show various anomalies. Neurotypical children similarly repeat words or talk to themselves, but their words are always appropriate to the scene. However, an autistic child's parroting does convey much meaning and is just a repeating of words heard from the ear. When they are talking to themselves, their eyes wander and seem strange.

So, I thought about why such behavior, senses, and language occur, what they mean, and how I can cure it.

First of all, in the physical development of autistic children, in most cases they are growing steadily. Even children with severe autistic symptoms who do not speak at all and struggle with incontinence will not die from autism. In other words, it can be said that it is a condition that does not directly impact whether an individual will live or die.

Put another way, it is the cerebrum, and whether dog or human, if you successfully remove the cerebrum, they can continue to live as long as the people around them give them food. Then, what is the job of the cerebrum? It is to catch changes in the environment, memorize necessary information, and help act appropriately according to each situation. It is meant to make it possible for one to better adapt to their surrounding environment, and what plays that role are the sensory center, the movement center, and the language center. I think that autistic children may have an abnormality in this part. Unfortunately, we do not yet know clearly why this abnormality occurs.

Although there are theories that say the mother's physical contact was insufficient or that the children were simply born that way, from past treatment cases I have come to hypothesize that it is the result of excessive stimulation of sounds and food to the growing brain of the child. Exposed to more stimulation than the brain can process, the cerebrum's normal functions begin to go haywire.

Until now, many people believed that these children lacked affection, communication, or effort on the part of their loved ones. But while they tried play therapy and group education, even if the children showed small changes in their behavior, there have been few who improved drastically.

On the other hand, as a result of attempting to reduce stimuli like television and food, abnormalities in the sensory and behavioral aspects suddenly disappear. From here, I have seen the progression of language comprehension, the manifestation of short speech, the disappearance of parroting, and the ability to participate in conversations. I surmised it was not a lack of stimulation, but rather an overexposure to stimulation.

The world today is very noisy, whether TVs or cars. When we live in it, we become accustomed to an extent and do not feel it is so noisy. But the child's brain in the process of growth reacts strongly to these stimuli. It sometimes becomes overstimulated to the point that the brain's function will go awry.

In particular, television continuously emits sound and images from morning till evening. In the process of children truly becoming able to remember things, although it is very important to talk to the child according to their current state and respond to their words and actions, TV unilaterally sends out sounds and images. Because of its one-directional nature, it is not useful for mastering words in the real sense.

Also, unlike during the war and postwar era, the city is full of sweets and drinks. Even when buying what the children want, it is not as though such purchases will make a dent in the family's wallet, so parents tend to get what their children ask for. On the other hand, we are inundated with marketing ploys urging that unless children get nutrition by consuming milk, meat, and eggs, they will not grow. However, harm caused by excessive overeating has begun to appear in various forms including obesity in children, and I think that it is time to think about the harm caused by too much food for autistic children.

Additionally, in the era of power shortage, I was disciplined to turn off the light often. But now it is fine to have a beaming light bulb on at night, and it is not considered a bad or wasteful action. We are running too far towards convenience and the biological rhythm of human beings is being destroyed. Also, in the case of autistic children, it is sound and food that mainly act as excessive stimuli, but the cerebrum is one entity, so if one part goes wrong, the other parts do as well. Therefore, I think that abnormality of various sensations and sleep are based on the same cause.

In this way, if you think of the cause as excessive stimulation, you can think of removing it as the cure. As mentioned earlier, by eliminating television, radio, records, cassette tapes, and music boxes, as well as limiting snacks and meal portions, turning off the light at night, and reducing certain stimuli, improvements will be made.

In other words, I think that it is not an issue on the psychological level such as a lack of love or physical contact, but rather an abnormality at the physiological level of the workings of the cerebrum.

With S, whom I mentioned earlier, we focused on eliminating television. Now, I would like to introduce "D," a child who has significantly improved since the summer of 1977 through newer methods such as quitting kindergarten, restricting their diet, and keeping the light off at night.

Case D

Born in May 1974. Has a sister two years younger. Male.

A letter to the guidance clinic, August 1977 *(Three years and three months)*

"We read your book which was recommended to us by a teacher in our neighborhood.

Even though I knew that my child was like this due to the influence of TV, I could not cut it out completely until now. However, for the past month, I have kept it off.

Though I was full of regret, feeling it was too late, I have picked up this pen to seek consultation on how to help him get better instead of lamenting the past.

I think he is a typical case of autism.

Currently three years and three months old.

Even if he is called, he shows no response (especially with strangers).

He lacks facial expressions and is not very active.

He cannot understand what I say.

His language acquisition has been slow.

Currently, he can say "bye-bye," "car," "bread," "red," "river," and "yes." He has an affinity towards objects with rules or patterns such as numbers, cars, and logos.

He often lies down and plays with his toy cars, abacus, and ruler.

It was around a year and a half ago that I began to think it strange, but people told me that he has some delay because he is a boy. I agreed to some extent, but thought it was unusual all the same.

When he turned two years old and still did not know words, we had a psychological examination at a public health center and saw a pediatrician at the university hospital, an ear, nose, and throat doctor, and a speech therapist.

As a result of the electroencephalogram (EEG), we were told he is intellectually disabled. He took a stimulant for six months, but as it did not work so much, we stopped giving it to him. I was advised to enroll him in a nursery at the health care center.

At the child consultation center, we were told he is autistic and were recommended weekly play therapy.

The psychiatry department of the education center also advised him to enroll in a nursery school because he is autistic.

Currently, play therapy once a week (from July).

On other days, nursery school in the mornings (from July).

He does not eat the school lunches, so I visit him at lunchtime to help him eat.

He is fine when he is playing freely on his own, but when he is put in a group he raises his voice. His kindergarten teacher also seems to have trouble interacting with him."

Guidance interview, September 1977 *(Three years and four months)*

[Mother's account]
Although he is calm at home, he wanders around a lot at nursery school.

The number of students in his class for two-year-olds reached fifteen on September 5th when eight more kids joined the group.

Since then, he has regressed and does not eat lunch even if I go.

At the time, the television at home was kept on for about fourteen hours a day from seven o'clock in the morning to nine o'clock at the night.

Since we completely cut out television in August, he has gradually stopped gazing blankly at the ceiling as he always used to do.

Until now, even when he was walking around outside, I was told that he looks like he is asleep. But nowadays, I am not told that as often.

On the other hand, these days he has become much more active.

He also screams and makes bizarre sounds.

When we go shopping, he goes off on his own and disappears.

[Behavioral observation]

- He has limited facial expressions and does not laugh.
- He was riding a toy car and running around the room, but soon after laid down on the floor and moved his minicar back and forth.
- He would also move his hips as though he were masturbating.
- He moves the toy cars and says "vroom!"
- He listens when his father and mother tell him to stand up or clean up the toys, but he does not respond when I call him.

[Diagnosis]

- Autism

[Guidance]

- Introduce "O," another child who has been receiving treatment at our guidance center for about a year. Compare them on the basis of the different treatments they have been receiving.
- D should take a break from the nursery school for a while.
- If possible, he should also stop play therapy.

September 1977 (Ten days after the initial consultation)
Telephone consultation

[From his mother]

After I took him out of the nursery school, he began to smoothly speak a lot of words. So, his father was elated and suggested we quit the nursery. However, the school says that since he has already started, he should continue.

They also offered to provide full support.

What should I do?

We also met O.

If it's possible to improve so much in just a year, I definitely want to try the treatments here.

[Guidance]

- Keep a diary.
- Go to the nursery school about once a week to show them his progress, and with their understanding, gradually stop going.

October 1977 *(Three years and five months)*

[Mother's account]

Although his pronunciation is not good, he can say more than ten words including "dog," "no," "dad," "train," "toy," "bag," "lighter," and "cider."

When we first turned off the television he was only able to say about four words, but in the last month he has shown drastic progress.

He shows more facial expressions, and his crying—which

sounded like a shrieking monkey—now sounds more like that of a child.

However, perhaps out of boredom, he often builds up spit in his mouth, sticks his fingers in his nose, or rattles the doors.

When we go out, he goes into this shop and that shop.

He loves sweet candy, and I often buy it for him.

He does not eat fruits and vegetables.

We quit nursery school at the end of September.

Although we tried play therapy after that, the clinic would play cassette tapes all day long and had many of his favorite toy cars, so we stopped going there as well.

These days, he sleeps well. He used to wake up in the middle of the night and stare at the night light for hours.

[Behavioral observation]

Height 93 centimeters, weight 15 kilograms.

- When I tried to measure his height, he saw the numbers on the scale and started wanting one for himself, making it hard to measure him.
- His facial expressions are not so different from before.
- He is close to being expressionless.
- To his mother, he would open a book and point, saying "Aah..."
- He also took her notebook and made sounds similar to the term "word."
- When holding his mini toy car, he laid down on the floor and moved it back and forth. When we took the car away,

he had a crying fit .

[Evaluation]

- Although speech is more evident than before, he is still restless.
- If you give him a toy car or a ruler, he will suddenly become quiet and calm.

[Guidance]

- Do not buy or give him sweets.
- Shorten the time spent outdoors.

November 1977 *(Three years and six months)*

[Mother's account]
It has been two-and-a-half months since we turned off the television.

He began to say words like "Chang (his sister)," "bye-bye," "shoes," "pupoon (spoon)," and "juju (juice)," but his facial expressions are still underdeveloped.

He hardly shrieks anymore.

His complexion, which was a blueish hue before, now has a redder tone.

He does not roll around, masturbate, or pick his nose as much as before.

I stopped giving him snacks.

He now has a greater appetite and eats well.

He used to run away at the mere sight of vegetables, but after about a week he started to eat them quite eagerly. However, the first week of refusing him snacks was a serious feat. He would point to the shelf and make a big fuss.

When he cried and screamed while grocery shopping, I told the cashier about our situation and never bought him snacks.

After a week of telling him "no," perhaps he began to understand as he stopped asking me to buy them.

However, he sometimes goes to other people's homes, walks around with their candy jars, and eats them. This is quite concerning.

These days, he has stopped pulling my hand.

Before, we used to take him out on drives a lot. Whenever he got in the car, he seemed satisfied and became quiet. Thinking he would be delighted, we drove around here and there.

If he cried, I took him for a drive.

When he cried at night, I took him for a drive.

[Behavioral observation]

- Although his complexion now has a redder tone, his eyes are still unfocused and he does not make eye contact.
- He is still expressionless.
- Holding a toy car, he'll say, "puka (supercar)."While pointing to a word in his mother's notebook, he'll say, "te (ten)" or "ree (three)."
- He has become increasingly active and runs around the

room yelling.

[Evaluation]

- In the past month his speech has improved, but his facial expressions and eyes still are not better.

[Guidance]

- Do not ride too much in the car.
- Reduce the portion of his meals.

December 1977 *(Three years and seven months)*

[Mother's account]

These days he often sticks to me, so his sister inevitably goes to their father,

Still, he and his sister both fight over my attention.

While I am on the phone, he pulls his sister's ears and causes a lot of mischief.

His attachment to calendars is still strong, and when he goes to someone's house he stares at them.

To people in stores, he demands that they lift him up and help him see while he counts "one, two, three..."

Although I reduced his meals, he has a tremendous appetite.

He wakes up when he hears the sound of breakfast being prepared.

He likes everything from apples to onions.

However, as a result, he ransacks the house and will lick even a container of miso.

[Behavioral observation]

Height 96.5 centimeters (increased by 3.5 cm in two months), weight 15.5 kilograms (increased by 0.5 kilograms in two months).

- His younger sister brought a dustpan and broom from the shoe rack. Seeing it, he opens the door of the shoe rack, takes out a shoe box, and pull out the shoes. When his father tells him "No," he clutches the shoes and runs away.
- He looks happy only at such times, but the rest of the time he looks lethargic.
- He brought a chair, stood on it, and pointed to the office calendar saying "Ah, ah, ah."
- He does not climb up on the panel.
- When asked, "Can you say bye-bye?," he used to turn the other way. Now, he can say "Bye."

[Evaluation]

- He is active but can have more energy.
- I hope his eyes become more focused.
- He has still not shown rapid progress in his speech.

[Guidance]

- Because he is growing taller, reduce his intake of meat, fish, eggs, and milk.

January 1978 *(Three years and eight months)*

[Mother's account]

The speech is improving a bit, but it is not enough.

He has learned the words "candy," "mouth," "tooth," "racker (rice cracker)," "pone (telephone)," "light," "yummy," "switch," "cake," "up," "snow," "hands," "opposite," "mama," "pee," and "piggy (piggyback)."

I do not know what language it is, but he speaks long sentences. This has been happening for about the last month.

He still likes calendars. When we go to the store, he looks at the calendars on the walls.

We spent New Year's quietly as his diet is restricted and we did not make New Year's dishes.

Every day he wakes up shouting for breakfast. Since he gets up at six o'clock in the morning and loudly demands for food, I get up early and prepare him breakfast so as not to disturb the neighbors.

He sleeps ten hours from eight o'clock in the evening to six o'clock in the morning.

He becomes lethargic if he sleep any longer.

At night, we keep the night light on as he does not like the dark.

[Behavioral observation]

Height 97.5 centimeters (increase by 1 cm), weight 15.5 kilograms (no change)

- He takes off his shoes and comes in.
- His facial expressions are still rather dull.
- However, when the telephone rings, he always turns towards the office.
- He says phrases that I do not understand.
- He spoke for quite a long time, and he seemed to be talking to himself.
- Approaching his mother, he requested a piece of paper. He wrote "10" with a pencil and said "ten." He cried in want of a medical chart recording paper, but when I said "No," he took his mother's notebook and began to draw lines to match the chart.
- He pointed outside and said, "ba (bus)" and "ruck (tow truck)."
- He freely flips through picture books and says "donuts" and "bread," but when I ask "What's this?," he does not reply.
- However, when his mother tells him to "Put that away," he will return the ruler he is holding.
- When she says "Let's go home.," he goes to the entrance while saying "Bye."

[Evaluation]

- Slow progress but not much improvement in his expressions and speech.

[Guidance]

- Turn off the night light.

February 1978 *(Three years and nine months)*

[Mother's account]

When we turned off the light at night after our last consultation, he cried for a couple of days and came to touch my and his father's face in the middle of the night.

Also, since it is dark in the house during the daytime, I used to keep the lights on all through the day. But when I stopped doing this, about a week later his words began to emerge suddenly and he started calling me "mommy."

His facial expressions have also gotten better.

Although I have not taught him much in particular, he has begun learning more and more and calls me over himself.

He has started saying long sentences such as "Mama, I want food.," "Nice jeans.," "Chang (sister), fidge (refrigerator), no good."

When asked "How old are you?," he answers, "Thwee (three years old)." However, when asked, "What's your dad's name?," he says "Papa."

When someone comes to visit, whether it is morning or noon he'll say, "Evening (Good evening)."

His strange habits have also started to disappear.

He has stopped moving boxes of tissue paper and slippers back and forth, and he does not gaze at calendars as much as before. However, he will count everything.

Although I still keep his diet restrictions, he does not want as much as before.

Even if I take him shopping, he does not want to buy that much.

However, when he goes to other people's houses, he wants snacks when he see them. I do not give any snacks at all.

He has stopped playing alone and he fights over everything with his sister.

Comprehension of words has improved, and he can be stopped from doing something with words alone.

[Behavioral observation]

Height 98 centimeters (increased by 0.5 centimeters), weight 16 kilograms (increased by 0.5 kilograms).

- He entered the room wearing an overcoat. He pulled out a chair and looked inside the office. When his mother said "Take your coat off," though he could not do it well, he put his hand on the buttons.
- He found the mandarin oranges inside the room. Wanting them, he pointed towards them, turned to his mother, and said, "Orange, orange!"
- He would stare at the calendar before, but today he does not even look at it.
- He pushed a cardboard box around the room saying, "Baba baba..."
- He showed his car to his mother and said "Caa (car?)."

- In this way, he speaks often but his pronunciation is bad, so it is difficult to understand him.
- While hopping around with his sister, he looked at her face and laughed delightedly.
- He laid down with a toy car and moved it back and forth, but quit immediately.
- He also let me measure his height and weight obediently and quietly today.
- I gave him the tape measure as he wanted it, but when I asked him if I could have it back, he returned it.
- His vague facial expressions disappeared, and even when he cried or laughed, it did not seem abnormal.

[Evaluation]

- In the past month, visible progress has finally been made.

[Guidance]

- Continue his meal restrictions as before.

March 1978 *(Three years and ten months)*

[Mother's account]

His vocabulary has increased very much and exceeds 200 words.

He says two or three-word sentences when making a request, but only offers one-word answers to my questions.

He talked to himself for a bit in January, but since his vocabulary started to increase in February he stopped.

His attachment to numbers has also diminished, but is not completely gone.

He plays pretend with his sister who is two years younger than him. They are almost like twins.

These days, he becomes violent and throws things if I do not give him immediate attention.

Perhaps because he does not eat between meals, he complains about a stomachache about once every three days after finishing his meals.

He asks me to give him a band-aid, and when I do, he says, "All better." and starts eating again. I do not give him any snacks whatsoever.

For a while I tried not to invite the neighborhood kids to our house, but after some months I invited one of the boys. Although he said "Come in!" and invited him to play, after about an hour he went back to playing alone.

[Behavioral observation]

Height 97.5 centimeters (decreased by 0.5 cm), weight 15.5 kilograms (decreased by 0.5 kilograms)

- His facial expressions have become natural without the awkward stiffness.
- His complexion is whiter.
- While riding a toy car, he runs around saying "Woo!"
- When he hears sirens sounding outside, he runs to the windows. When his mother asks "What is it?," he replies,

"Ambulance."

- Although his pronunciation is not yet clear, he says words accompanied by actions.
- He has stopped talking to himself.

[Evaluation]

- He seems to be in a stable state.
- His face looks better and his vocabulary has increased.

[Guidance]

- Give him some snacks.
- Go out for about an hour a day.

April 1978 *(Three years and ten months)*

[Mother's account]

Despite his pronunciation, I have become able to understand most of his words.

When speaking from himself he can form sentences, but he still only gives single-word answers to questions.

He calls himself "He (Me?)".

I give him two rice crackers at nine o'clock in the morning and at three o'clock in the afternoon.

I reduce the portion of his lunch by that amount.

After I started giving him snacks, his abdominal pain healed.

Breakfast is served at six o'clock. He eats a moderate portion of rice served in a children's bowl, miso soup, and no side dishes.

For lunch, he eats a bowl of noodles.

Dinner is a bowl of rice and some side dishes.

He always says, "Mama, look at me!," and he has frequently started asking "What is this?" from around March.

However, when I try to teach him about something, he gets annoyed.

Although he reacts to my words, if another person talks to him he ignores them.

He is not shy around strangers and he goes up to anyone.

When out for a long time, he starts to get tired and becomes expressionless.

Even if I talk to him, he does not respond.

Even if I put him on my bicycle, he would seem absent-minded.

However, he likes to look outside the window and wants to go to where other children are.

[Behavioral observation]

Height 98 centimeters (increase by 0.5 cm), weight 16 kilograms (increase by 0.5 kilograms)

- His facial expressions are still stiff, but nothing stands out as out of the ordinary.
- He carries a lot of picture books and says "Mine" without sharing them with other children.
- He often says, "Mommy, look at me!"

- He holds a toy car and runs away as another child approaches for fear of getting it taken away.
- When I say "There it goes.," while he watches the cars outside, he says "It goes."
- When I asked, "What's that?" he answered correctly, "Bus."
- He says "Pee," goes to the toilet by himself, and comes back.
- When he asked for paper, I handed him a sheet and watched him draw lines like earthworms.
- During this time, there was no reaction even if I talked to him.
- When other children came in with sweets, he immediately made a fuss because he wanted them.

[Evaluation]

- His vocabulary has increased and his pronunciation has improved.
- His reaction to speech is still dull.

[Guidance]

- There is no need to speak to him excessively.
- Answer him when he talks to you.

Chapter 6

Role a of Kindergarten Teacher

Seek Progress Before Entering Group Environments

Initially, autism was thought to be an emotional disorder that could be treated with play therapy. But children who actually take play therapy and manage to live as part of society is said to be one in every 100, and from around 1973, the belief that collective childcare is better has become stronger. Thus, autistic children have increasingly begun to enter nursery schools and kindergartens nationwide.

In response to that, kindergarten and nursery school teachers have also enthusiastically devoted themselves to producing good results. However, many of them wonder if what they are doing is enough, and become fatigued from handling unpredictable autistic children.

From personal experience, I have noticed that children who went to ordinary kindergartens and nursery schools show more progress than children who received play therapy. For this reason, we have recommended enrollment as much as possible and appealed actively to kindergartens and nursery schools to accept autistic children. However, in July of 1977, I began to question collective childcare when I encountered four children who got worse after starting school.

Also, in February 1977, when Luna Children's Consultation Office was opened, more autistic children than expected came for consultations from all over the country. Among them were children who had already been in group environments for two or three years, some who had even been going to nursery school from eight or ten months after birth.

In July of 1977, I tried analyzing the records of thirty-one children who had been attending kindergartens and nursery schools until the previous year. As a result, I encountered a few surprising facts.

With the exclusion of one case, none of the ten children who entered nursery school before the age of three showed linguistic progress. Most were unable to speak at all, and even if they knew some words to make requests, they were not at the level where they could have conversations. Even among children who entered at the age of three (three-year child-care), only five children showed improvements. Eight of them showed no progress, revealing that most children do not get better. The children who did get better had already been able to repeat words or commercials at the time of enrollment, knowing how to vocalize words they heard by ear. Children who entered school without speech were unable to acquire words even after over a year.

From the age of four, children who memorized words from commercials suddenly became able to have conversations. In particular, S, who entered nursery school one year and seven months after eliminating television *(see page 125)* has advanced to where it he can be regarded as almost "normal."

However, the children who could not speak much at the time of enrollment are still unable to utilize language. Taking this into consideration, I felt that it would rather be negative to put an autistic child without the ability to speak in a group setting.

Insisting that families "turn off the television" and producing positive outcomes was my way of reducing sound stimulation from the environment, but when I actually went to a nursery school or kindergarten, there were lots of children and teachers. Their voices were quite noisy, and there was a lot of commotion from the sound of records, musical instruments, and toys bumping against each other. Because the brain of autistic children protects its brain cells from excessive sound stimulation by dulling its susceptibility, it is imperative to first place them in a quiet environment and alleviate their symptoms. It is necessary to raise the sensitivity of their brain to the point where they can distinguish disparate sounds that enter their ears. It is a mistake to think that because they have not yet acquired speech, it would be better to put them in a nursery school or kindergarten with a lot of verbal stimulation.

Why did I not realize something so simple? Why did I single-mindedly believe that collective childcare was the solution? I had a moment of deep regret.

I now understand why I have been told that autism cannot be treated. Thus far, autism treatment has revolved around repeatedly exposing autistic children to strong stimuli, but there is no way this will help them improve.

Compared to children who go to kindergartens and nursery schools in general, children who go to school facilities for children with disabilities have poor language development. I once met a child who stopped speaking after going for two or three years, despite having been able to before she was admitted. At first I wondered why, but I have now been able to solve that mystery as well.

Schools and facilities specializing in working with children with disabilities have more teachers than typical kindergartens, so they are able to individually work with children on how to tie their shoes, practice saying their vowels, and eat when they refuse to do so. However, it seems like these tenacious efforts have actually brought about results that exacerbate the state of the child. While they may learn lifestyle habits that were repeatedly taught to them, language acquisition does not develop normally. So, I understood that it is necessary to discern quite strictly the appropriate time to put these children into collective childcare.

Then, as we look at the entrants in 1977 and 1978, children who enrolled after removing television for over a year and a half, could talk with anyone, and improved overall to the level of neurotypical children showed almost no problems even in kindergarten thereafter.

In April and May at the beginning of the school year, they might cry, not be able to stand up smoothly, and not know how to greet others, but any child who is placed in a group environment for the first time will cry or have trouble playing with others. Even if their teacher says they are restless, by June they should be acting similar to other children.

However, if it has been less than a year for a child after turning off the television, even if they can have everyday conversations and have no significant problems at home, there are cases where they will enter kindergarten and manifest issues such as entering rooms without permission, not being able to walk in a line, not eating meals, not taking naps, and going outside with bare feet.

Even in the months of June and July, they will struggle to work in groups and stand out. In the autumn athletic meetings, they might be the only student to be pulled by the teacher when running in races. Overall, they will have trouble fitting into group life smoothly.

Also, in terms of language, they will struggle to understand abstract concepts such as colors, numbers, opposites, and cause and effect.

That's why, in order to put them into a group environment, they should first turn off the television for at least a year and a half. It is not until they are able to speak well, have rich expressions, and be calm to the point where strangers will think them no different from neurotypical children will I advise them to enter a nursery school. I carefully examine each child and offer advice according to their individual situation.

Important Points of Childcare

However, in reality, there are a lot of autistic children who enter schools in a state of restlessness and no speech. There are a lot of kindergarten teachers who do not know what to do although they have accepted them into their facilities.

From a standpoint of someone who had asked nursery schools and kindergartens to accept autistic children, I myself visited various facilities to observe the state of the children and have discussions with the nursery school teachers. From that experience, I have found some points to keep in mind when caring for autistic children.

Numerous childcare reports are also being issued by the schools and children who have improved very much through group childcare have also appeared. But from here, I would like to make some suggestions through the examples of successes and failures from the standpoint of a psychological evaluator.

More Than One Class Teacher

Children with autism often do not follow instructions and move around freely. If you try to tend to them individually while also teaching a lot of other children, you will become exhausted. Therefore, if possible, schools should assign multiple teachers to each classroom and have one of them oversee the autistic children.

However, in this case, if you fix the role to a specific person, other teachers will get the impression that the care of the autistic children has been entrusted to one teacher. They will not get involved and, as a result, the autistic children will not receive the full support of the school. If this occurs, the teacher in charge of looking after the autistic children will only be able to keep their eyes on them. This may feel like a tremendous responsibility for the teacher, and the children will also feel less a part of the class.

Additionally, the other children will have less opportunities to interact directly with their autistic classmates for fear of getting in the way of the teacher in charge. As a result, the benefits of collective childcare will be diminished.

In a similar way, it is not good to have their mothers stay with them at school. It may be inevitable if the child becomes extremely upset at being away from their mother, but schools should not take in autistic children under the condition that they will be accompanied by their mother for the first one or two years. This will not help the children get better.

It is ideal to have multiple teachers in charge of a class and have one of them focus on caring for the autistic students. While doing so, they can facilitate their involvement with the rest of the class. When the child has started to settle into their new environment, the teacher can then leave their side and lead them to interact further with the other kids.

Do Not Coddle, Discipline Properly

There is a wide belief that autism is an emotional disorder caused by the parents' rejection of the child, and therefore if parents do not refuse any of their children's requests and approach with an accepting attitude, the children will open up their heart and be cured of autism. There are many nursery schools with a policy of acceptance.

However, what we prohibit for other children should be prohibited for children with autism as well. For example, actions that inconvenience others such as removing all the shoes from the shoe rack, cutting the drawstrings of the other children's bags, leaving the faucet on in the bathroom, and pulling out all the toilet paper should be strictly prohibited. Even if they beg to do it, we should hold their hands and feet and adamantly refuse.

We will guide them to do things by themselves as much as possible, such as changing their clothes, putting on their shoes, and organizing their bags, even if it takes time. In that case, it is better not to force them to repeat it many times in an attempt to make them remember. Tell them one or two times, help out as needed, and if they still cannot do it, try again the next day.

There was one kindergarten where the teacher would grab the child's cheeks and force eye contact, but the moment they took their hands away, the child turned sideways. This strategy will not truly help them to make eye contact. It is best to be patient and take things slow while maintaining an appropriate distance.

Talk to Them Individually

In nursery settings, it is common for teachers to talk to a large number of children at once, but autistic children often have trouble understanding. In such situations, if you go to the child and say the same thing again in a low voice, they may understand and take action.

With neurotypical children it is better to have a loud voice, but with autistic children, they will listen more if you speak slowly in a small voice. In addition, they will understand better if they are given real objects to learn from as much as possible.

There are some children who can read letters, are interested in numbers, and are seemingly smarter than other children, but in terms of speech, they are very inferior. They may not understand simple phrases like "Go there!" or "Line up!" Words related to daily life must be taught one by one while accompanied by action.

Be as Quiet as Possible

There are many children in kindergartens and nursery schools, so some noise cannot be avoided by any means, but some kindergartens are relatively quiet while others are filled with shouting children, the sound of instruments, and the sound of speakers.

Regarding the structure of the buildings, reinforced concrete is bad, but wooden structures are quiet. Children's voices resound well in a building made of reinforced concrete and vinyl-tile floors, making it very noisy. Reinforced concrete may be more common to prevent fire hazards, but I think that materials with high sound absorption should be used for floors, ceilings, and walls so that the children's voices do not reverberate.

In addition, when it comes to mammoth kindergartens with two to three hundred students, microphones are often used. However, we want to lower the volume as much as possible so that it can be heard only within the necessary range. We should also reduce sound stimulation as much as possible by turning off TV and records. Organs and percussion instruments should also be minimized, and lessons should switch to teaching nursery rhymes.

If the teacher's voice is made as small as possible, children will also listen quietly. Normally, the teacher always tends to talk in a loud voice so that everyone hears her, but then the children will get louder so that the teacher will hear them.

Autistic children should be put in a quiet environment as much as possible. By encouraging speech and interactions within that environment, their symptoms will alleviate and comprehension will enhance.

There are also school buses that play music tapes and radio, but we should ask the driver to stop playing them. Some children spend up to two hours on the bus every day so it is not good.

The Mental Age of Autistic Children

Autism has mainly been considered an emotional disorder up until now, but looking at adults with autism, it greatly resembles intellectual developmental disorder.

I believe that they are born normal, but autistic children who are unable to become successfully treated will have a severe delay of mental development when they are older.

Furthermore, if you actually work with autistic children, I think that it will be useful to know how the child corresponds to the mental age of neurotypical children when establishing their childcare goals. Although it is a rough classification here, I tried to show the mental age according to the symptoms of autistic children. Regardless of the actual age of the child, this is meant to dictate symptoms as clues. When evaluating how much achievement has been made through childcare, this can be used as a guideline on how much their mental age has increased. Here, the mental age of zero years includes zero months after birth to eleven months after birth. The same goes for one and two-year-olds.

Mental age: Zero years old

- Even if you call their name from behind, they do not turn around.
- They do not make eye contact.
- They will pick up anything and put it in their mouth.
- They will not look for their mother even when she is gone.
- Even if they see food, they do not eat on their own.
- They step on everything from toys to books.
- They will enter a random room or go outside by themselves.
- They go outside barefoot.

- Even if banned, they will climb up on desks and play around with telephones, faucets, doors, or other people's bags.

Mental age: One year old

- When gathered in a group, they will not sit still and will go off on their own.
- They will not play with other children and will be isolated.
- When they want someone to do something, they will not make a verbal request but will take their hand and try to make them do it.
- They can say requests such as "Potty" or "Juice."
- They repeat words back.
- When called by their name, they can raise their hand and reply "Yes."
- During meals, they cannot wait and will begin eating first. They might also take their favorite foods from other children's plates.

Mental age: Two years old

- They will blend in with others when among a large group of children.
- They will be able to play simple games even if they are a tempo off.
- They will be able to sit down in their seat. Their selfish behavior will decrease.
- They can point correctly to questions such as "Where are

your eyes?" or "Where are your feet?"

- When asked "What is this?," they can answer correctly about the things they use every day (bags, shoes, chairs) even if they are asked by a stranger.
- They can have simple conversations such as "Give me scissors!," "Where is it?," and "It's over there." They can communicate with others about daily matters and will not struggle as much to convey their thoughts.
- They can go to the toilet by themselves, even if they fail occasionally.
- They can wear their pants on their own.
- Even if they spill somewhat, they can eat on their own with other children.
- They can hang up their bag or change their clothes without the help of others.

The classification given here indicates whether a child's mental age is zero or one year old. Once they can reach the mental age of two, I think that the childcare for autistic children can be regarded as successful. From here on forward, I will speak according to the same standards and policies as the childcare of neurotypical children.

Chapter 7

The Current "Treatments" of Autism

Currently, autism is not well-understood in regards to its actual condition or cause. But it cannot be left alone, so many attempts have been made to alleviate the symptoms. Although it seems that various hypotheses are made from various perspectives, there are still many things that are not understood and that contradict our theories. Our staff go through trial and error and desperately try to tackle these issues. It seems that is the current situation.

I wanted to see directly with my own eyes what autistic children are like, how they think, and what kind of treatment is being done, so I went to visit facilities here and there. I would like to introduce some of them and share my impressions.

Autism Ward

In June 1973, I went to visit the autism ward of the metropolitan mental psychiatric hospital for children. I heard about the autism ward a long time ago, so I thought if I went there I would be able to see typical autism cases. I was very much interested in what kind of treatment they were doing.

It was past three o'clock in the afternoon on a cold, rainy day when I arrived at the ward after receiving a brief explanation. That day was bathing day, and the children had just finished their baths. It was their free time in the afternoon. The ward was divided into two, one for small children under preschool and another for older children of elementary school age. The wards were mixed-gender.

We first entered the younger children's ward and went into the cafeteria. Several low desks like those at nursery school were lined up and cleaned. There were also pretty paper cutouts on the wall and the names and age of the children on origami. It was not time to eat, so of course there were no children. The door was locked so that the children could not enter arbitrarily. We were led into the day room and told, "The children are over here." It was a quite large, boarded room, but I was surprised to see that it was extremely clean.

The floor was shiny, and in the room was one children's bicycle, one tricycle, one set of alphabet blocks, one old magazine, and one black-and-white television that was turned on. The window was beautiful, but fitted with lattice and the door leading to the courtyard was locked so they could not go out. In the cupboard were stuffed toys, hula hoops, and other toys, but the doors were nailed down out of reach of the children to prevent them from taking them out freely. Because the hallway leading to the bedrooms was also locked, the children could not go anywhere except this day room. Only one nurse was in the day room attending to the children. The other three or four workers seemed to be recording charts in the office and did not come out.

I entered this room and looked around for a moment. To be honest, I was left speechless at its cleanliness. How could a room with a group of children be so clean…? Most households with one or two children are scattered with books, toys, and sometimes even tableware on the floor... There was nothing messy here.

As for the children, some were sitting in front of the TV, one was flipping through the channels, one was playing with building blocks, while another was showing the magazine to the nurse and pointing at something. They each played individually without talking or playing with the others. Someone said, "It's a silent world here.," and it was true that you could not hear anything except for the voices on TV. Even when we talked to them, of course they did not respond. But everyone had a good physique and looked normal and very cute.

Then, we were guided to the bedrooms. There were four clean beds arranged in every room and a box for personal items under each of them. There was nothing else. "We store their other belongings here," the staff said as she opened the door of the storage in the hallway. Of course, the children could not open this door either.

As this was a facility for autistic children, this may be natural as a matter of course, but it was too clean and too well arranged compared with the visiting and accommodation facilities of intellectually disabled children I had observed before. This may have been because it was a "hospital" and not a "facility," but usually the floor is a *tatami* mat, futons are laid out every evening, and personal items are stored in low, easily reachable drawers and cupboards. Normally there is no lock on the door, much less a locked partition between the dining room, bedrooms, and the day room. Even at the visiting and accommodation facility of intellectually disabled children I took a tour of about a month ago, the children freely pulled out books and put them all over the floor. They also brought drawing paper and crayons from somewhere after saying, "Let's draw!" However, at this autism ward, nothing could be done without permission.

Next, I went to the older children's ward on the opposite side. We could see inside through the lattice door. The woman showing us around said, "Because the construction is the same, everything else is generally the same. The kids in here are bigger, so I don't know what they might do to you. Whatever they do, I can't take responsibility. Do you still want to go inside?" She repeated this a few more times. Since we wanted to see the children, we said, "We don't mind, please let us inside." I had her unlock the door and show us into the day room.

Once inside the room, some of the children ran over and tried to take someone's glasses, while others pulled our hair and even tried to rip someone's scab off. Again, on the floor, there were a couple of baskets with toys in it, such as a telephone set and a bat. Some old tires were on the floor and the black-and-white television was turned on. In this room, the TV was kept in the back of the lattice door so that the channel could not be changed. There were two or three children who could speak a little here, but they were easy conversations like "No!" in response to me putting out my hand and asking, "Can I have that?" From the corner, I heard a strange, high-pitched voice. When I went to go see, a boy about ten years old had his penis out and was masturbating. When we looked closely, another boy around the same age was also masturbating behind the shelf. When we stood there whispering, the woman who was in the day room came running and scolded the children: "Hey! You're doing it again!"

The cuteness was gone from the faces of the older children and their eyes were dispassionate. There was no tightness in their face and their eyes glowed intensely only when they tried to attack people. It was a bad feeling. However, their bodies were as large as neurotypical children, and their hands and feet also looked normal.

According to our guide, they have a different program every day, and one staff member attends to one child as they move their body, play games, and memorize words. But, due to the limited time we had there, we could not see these treatment programs. Therefore, I do not think we saw everything there was to see there, but I was forced to wonder if this was an environment suitable for child development. At some point during the day they may be able to receive a rich "treatment," but in the ten hours they spend after waking up in the morning, they have no choice but to be in the limited space of the dining room or day room. Moreover, there are very few ways that the children can freely play. Children sometimes break objects and get muddy, but as they try new things, they will grow through tremendous amounts of experience. I thought that to be in an environment that is too clean with nothing to do would be a big detriment to their development.

Our guide repeatedly told us, "Stable children are encouraged to stay overnight at home as much as possible to maintain their connection with their family. The children you see here now are mostly those with heavy symptoms. It would be unfair for you to judge our treatment strategies just from what you've seen." However, the guide was an office clerk and said that she could not answer our questions about their treatment policies and how they evaluate the progress of the children.

I coincidentally met a nurse who worked at this hospital in July 1974. When I shared my experience with her, she said, "I do not know how the doctor describes it, but we do not think that we are doing treatment here. One of the first things we tell the families is that they should not expect their autistic child to get better by being hospitalized here. In actuality, since it is impossible to care for them at home, we are accommodating them here. In the beginning we did not have so many partitions, but they would hide in a corner, relieve themselves, and knead their own excrement. We had to clean up after them all day long, which is why we set up the partitions. Recently, the children who come to be hospitalized have been showing increasingly severe symptoms, so it really is tough."

At One Laboratory

I visited a laboratory famous for the treatment of autism in the southwestern part of Tokyo in September 1974. This laboratory seems to have been made about ten years ago, mainly for the treatment of autistic children. It seemed to be a refurbished private house with rooms connected by maze-like corridors. There were a number of playrooms, a room with a pool, a bathroom, a room for group nurseries, and a break room for staff. There was also a simple playroom like a classroom, but there were some other playrooms equipped with stairs and tunnels, and the room with the pool also had special lighting. In the group nursery rooms, it was unusual to see a toilet attached to each room, but lattice was attached to the window of the second floor.

As we went in the afternoon, the children in group nursery (not only autistic children but also various disabled children and neurotypical children) were not there. Instead, there were five children receiving individual play therapy. They were all infants from four to six years old. They each used a single room with one therapist to each child, and the therapists talked and played with the children.

In the garden there was a swing. A therapist was pushing a girl of about six years old on the swing for a long time. The swing had a bar at chest height so that the child could not fall. The girl only said, "Aaaah......" while spreading and shaking her hands. They did this for about twenty minutes.

A boy about four years old was accompanied by a male therapist who wrote the kanji of the words that the child said. When the child went down the slide, he said, "That was fun, wasn't it?" This boy was a child who did not like having people around, so for the time being, we were told it was important to let him feel that even if a therapist is present he does not get in the way. Eventually, they will help him see that it is convenient and pleasant to have people there. Once this is achieved, he will come to seek people from himself. However, he went out to the garden every fifteen or twenty minutes to pee in the sandbox. I was worried that it may be a case of frequent urination....

In the bathroom while filling up the bathtub, a girl went in alone with a therapist at her side. After a while, the child got up out of the bath, wore clothes, and started playing in the room with the pool. Because it was cold there was no water in the pool, but they put water like clay in bottles and empty mayonnaise tubes and played with that.

The children did not speak much and the therapists did not actively talk to them either. Even when one of the children brought the tube containing the dirty water to her mouth, the therapist did not stop them. However, I was relieved to see that she noticed the strange smell of the water and decided not to drink it.

In the biggest room, a pretty big boy around six to seven years old had stripped down to his shirt and was walking back and forth in the room. Although a male therapist was with him, he only stood and watched and did not instruct him to wear pants. There was another child who was lying on the knee of their therapist while eating biscuits during snack time, as well as a child who was lying on a mattress while eating.

It seemed that play therapy was carried out for one hour

and a half each time in this way. The frequency of the sessions depend on each individual child, and if done twice a week, it will cost 20,000 yen monthly. When done three times a week it will cost 30,000 yen a month.

When asked what the children who finished treatment here are doing, they answered, "They usually enroll in a school with a one to two-year delay. We choose children who we believe would be OK to go to school and adapt well. However, there are also many children who cannot attend school. One third of the children continue to be treated once a week at another place, and another third of the children we do not know if the treatment was effective and currently seem to be at home."

"However, in the last couple of years, parents have become more enthusiastic about enrollment, and an increasing number of them now send their children to school once they have reached school age. But, in some cases, there are children who escape from windows, climb up to the roof, become frustrated, and seem to become worse than before. It is not as though they will easily get better if placed among neurotypical children."

In response to the question, "What do children who stay at home do? What do children who are treated here do when they do not come here?," they answered, "Small children who are often at home with their mothers can be mischievous but also play well. But with bigger children, many of them do not do anything which is worrisome. However, it is dubious whether pulling these children out of their own world and putting them in groups will make them happy...."

What concerned me about this facility was their emphasis on "acceptance," which I thought might be another way of saying they are compliant with the children. They are desperate not to be an inconvenience to the children, and they rack their brains over how to be liked by them while constantly chasing after them. I think it's funny to interpret behaviors such as getting naked and playing on a swing for a long time as though there is something meaningful behind those actions.

Interpreting such socially unacceptable and simple acts as meaningful and playing with them does not help the children to progress. I doubt whether these children can distinguish between play and real-life situations. Also, I cannot agree with their reluctance to send them to schools and their belief that depending on the child, it is better for them to let them stay in their own bubble without joining groups. Humans cannot live by themselves, and in order to become a good member of society, is not it necessary to learn the techniques to be able to live as a member of a group as well?

At Kindergarten

The L Kindergarten in Musashino City in Tokyo is famous for accepting children with autism, and applicants wishing to attend come from Tokyo to as far away as Shikoku and Kyushu.

In 1974, there were about 800 neurotypical children and 154 children with autism, 950 students in all to create a mammoth kindergarten.

The neurotypical children are, of course, local children, but for the autistic children, commuting an hour one way is regarded as close. They come from Kanagawa, Chiba and Saitama prefectures. Some children even spend seven hours round-trip to commute from Yamanashi prefecture, taking a bullet train from Toyohashi. It is a daily event, so it is tough for both the parents and children. Those who cannot commute every day rent an apartment near the kindergarten and live a double life. Of course, they cannot leave the children there alone, so the mothers join them. Families from neighboring prefectures can go home on Saturdays and Sundays, but those who live farther away can only return during summer vacation, winter break, and spring vacation. The family may be able to bear it for the sake of their child, but it is seriously tough.

There are older children who have reached school age from three to about ten years old, but as the treatment shows its effects little by little, they recently seem to be focused on admitting three to four-year-old children.

Here, in the first year or so, they start off by creating classes of ten autistic children. When they think that they are ready, they assign two to three autistic children to a class of neurotypical children. Fast children may be assigned to a class for neurotypical students in about half a year, but in some cases, they are not assigned even after one year and remain in the class for autistic children.

It is said that children who are assigned to the class of

neurotypical children are not treated special and are handled like other children, but from my observations, there were few autistic children who were able to act at the same level as the other children. Some kids only stood with drumsticks in hand while the rest of the class struck a small drum in time to the music. During gym class they do not memorize the dance routines completely, so they imitate the other children but is always one step behind. They might also not enter the classroom unless pushed inside by another classmate. However, there are some children who can explain their work properly, saying "This is a train, this is a pantograph..." These children with solid language development are typically very lively.

The treatment policy here is completely different from the policy of acceptance and physical contact adopted in personal play therapy. Like with the neurotypical children, the autistic kids are scolded when they misbehave, are not served their lunches unless they wash their hands and have a seat, and are not given what they want just because they cry and make a commotion. The principal emphasized the importance of getting them to have conversations, and mentioned that it does not matter whether they can make eye contact or not. Some children come out of the classroom but are not forcibly pulled back. As long as they are playing in the garden, they are free to go where they please. Even if there is a child who is panicking and making noise, they do not act surprised. They say with a straight face, "If we ignore them, they'll stop doing it after the first or second time."

The classes for autistic children are not taught in a special way either. The teacher calls their name and makes them respond. They will draw circles and triangles on the blackboard and explain, "This is a circle. What other things are a circle?" to get them to name various objects. They draw, sing, and sing along to the organ while singing painting songs. The teachers try very hard, but while some children are eager to join, others are not. But, it was quiet for the number of students and there seemed to be relatively few children leaving their seats.

However, this kindergarten is not without problems.

It is nice that they have increased their capacity to accommodate the growing number of applicants, but now they do not have enough space, and since 1974, the students have been divided into three buildings. In particular, the third building which was newly built in 1974 is a shabby thing like a barrack school just after the end of the war. Though it is a temporary location, it is built with plywood boards and is cold in winter. The garden is muddy and the slide is made of wood, so mothers' gripe when their kids come back with holes in their trousers every four to five days. Here, there were autistic children who entered in 1974 and those who reached school age, but because of the separate buildings, they have no interactions with the neurotypical children.

Next, there is the matter of money. In the year 1974, the admission fee was 120,000 yen and the monthly tuition 25,000 yen. Besides this, it costs 2,000 yen for school lunches and 2,500 yen to ride the school bus. If there is an overnight camp it will incur more costs, and students must buy castanets and drum sticks, uniforms, hats, smocks, and bags. Needless to say, the school costs a lot of money .

Families who live relatively nearby can send their kids to school and return home, but for those living farther away, the mothers might wander around a nearby shopping district to wait and have lunch, adding onto the transportation expenses and tuition. As mentioned earlier, those from afar will sacrifice a lot of time, money, and energy in the form of hours spent on commuting or mothers and fathers living separately to rent a house near the kindergarten.

We also cannot ignore the emotional sacrifices made by the siblings of the children as well as the parents who may run into issues because of this. I could not help but think that if we can accept these children at every kindergarten and nursery school, we would not have to pay such sacrifices.

I asked about the children who graduated from here. The graduates in 1973 were forty-one students: twenty-two from ordinary classes, fifteen from special classes, and four from the disabled children's school. There were more graduates from the regular classes.

However, I was disappointed a bit when I saw N at the school for disabled children in September 1974. She had graduated this kindergarten. N entered L Kindergarten at the age of four, received education as an autistic child for one year, and was assigned to the class for neurotypical children in April at the age of five because she began to speak. Thus, for one year she was educated alongside the neurotypical children.

In April 1973, her year of school enrollment came, but as it was thought that it would be impossible, she was given permission to suspend school for one year to go to L Kindergarten for another year. All other neurotypical children had graduated and gone to elementary school, so she once again joined the class for autistic children. Here, the classes are divided into four (A, B, C, D) according to the degree of intellectual development, but N was assigned to class C because she had not progressed much.

Although the mother searched for other options, it was not easy to find a place that would accept her comfortably, so they decided to put her into this school for disabled children in April 1974. About L Kindergarten she said, "The principal said that she had started to speak, and if she repeatedly practiced each sound of words like 'goodbye', she will become able to say them. But, it is doubtful whether you can say if that really is a word. They were not even allowed to do the athletic meet with the neurotypical children, and when her turn came, she was separated from the group. When she was in her third year, she didn't even get changed for the meet and just came home with the goody bag. The parents of autistic children often end up feeling small…"

N has a large physique and well-structured face, but she cannot speak clearly. When changing clothes, if she struggles to pull up the zipper on the side of her skirt, she will go up to other people to have them do it. However, she will not vocalize her request. When I talk to her, she looks intently at my face, but that is all she does. She does not leave the classroom to walk around outside, and she is quiet. On her way home, she would walk while touching the hedges, but she would wait when told to do so by her mother.

Although it depends on the state of the child at the time of admission, as a child who joined the class of the older neurotypical children because she began to exhibit speech, the current state of N is not good enough. Children who were suddenly placed in an ordinary nursery school among neurotypical children show more progress in terms of language. This is not mentally easy for the kindergarten teachers, but the children certainly get better.

Currently, I think that the strategies of L Kindergarten are inevitable, but I think that autistic children should be accepted at typical nurseries and kindergartens as soon as possible.

Daycare at a University Hospital

I was able to visit the daycare of the university hospital that I had been wanting to see in November 1974. Here, they had three groups for daycare: one that met once a week and two that met twice a week, all from ten o'clock in the morning to three o'clock in the afternoon for five hours a day. Each group had about ten children, and they were led by a kindergarten teacher and a male clinical psychologist.

There were three large nurseries. They used the one towards the front of the building with the desks for roll call, changing, and meals, and the room in the middle for gymnastics, singing, and group activities. There were trampolines and swings in the back that they also used during playtime.

Along with autistic children, there were also children with Down's syndrome and epilepsy, but autistic children were the most common.

One therapist attends to each child, and they dance together and give individual guidance. During guidance, the children go to another room and learn face-to-face with their therapist.

I saw a boy of three years and ten months who was diagnosed with "exercise aphasia." When he was told to "open the curtain" he could open the curtain, and when he was asked "Where is your eye?" he could point it out. But his speech was limited to "ah" (meaning "yes"), but no other words could be said. For this child, the therapist lined up glue, scissors, ballpoint pens, and other real objects alongside pictures of cats, fountain pens, and caramel on the sofa and asked questions like, "Please take the scissors and caramel." The child also imitated his therapist and practiced drawing lines from one edge of a paper to the other with crayons.

Meal time was hard. There was a child who tried to drink milk before they were passed out to everyone else, a child who cried and refused to eat, and another child who did not want to pick up his fork by himself. The therapists had to go to each child to encourage and feed them. The therapists also had lunch in the same room, but I felt eating was the last of their concerns. Of course, they have no lunch break.

The treatment policy here is rather an emphasis on acquiring lifestyle habits and learning, and they do not coddle the children. There was a girl who had kept crying for about an hour, but they did not try to make her happy. When a child climbed up onto a desk, they scolded him. If a child gets up from their seat, they will catch them and pull them back. They deny the view that autistic children have "special talent," which is the opposite approach of the previously mentioned laboratory.

The cost for treatment twice a week was about 15,000 yen a month, but because there is no official program, the burden of providing the therapists' labor costs falls greatly on the parents. It was said they were also promoting the movement to finally be able to run on public expenses.

The feature here is that one-on-one therapy is included in addition to the main group guidance. They were doing a treatment method called operant conditioning, but was only in the form of rewarding a child with a cup of juice when they accomplish an assignment, or putting children with short attention spans in a small room called the "teaching booth" to work with them there. So, I did not think there was any special technique. To this extent, I thought that it would be sufficient to enroll in general nurseries and kindergartens, but the problem is personnel expenses.

We watched two movies from "Autism of Children" which

included scenes at the daycare there. The first one was made three years ago, and there were scenes in which children who were three years old during the filming of the first movie were shown as six-year-olds in the second. It was deeply intriguing.

Children who in the beginning were only interested in the flowing and swirling of water were shown one year later after receiving treatment at the daycare. They were filmed dancing with the therapists and other children and holding their hands. There were also scenes of them at kindergartens and schools, playing with other children and doing gymnastics. A girl who could only slowly move her hand in front of her face at the age of three danced together with others at age six, smiling and expressing joy on her face.

However, upon putting only these children in a room or ceasing to make an effort to interact with them, you will see that they will not cooperate with each other and play, or search for toys to play with on their own. Instead, they will go back to focusing on their own activities.

Although there is certainly progress, if compared with a neurotypical child, the difference is tremendous. I was left with a feeling of dissatisfaction at whether these treatments were enough, and whether further progress could be made…

Class for Special Needs Children

From around 1971, the special needs class of which there were only a handful in regions throughout Japan began to be seen more frequently in cities and districts. Children who until then could not go to school even after reaching school age became able to attend thanks to these special classes.

These classes often offer special support services. During most days of the week, students attend the normal or special classes, and while remaining enrolled in their homerooms, go to the special needs class once or twice a week. Depending on the school, there might be children who only attend the special needs class, children who attend both their homeroom classes and special needs classes, and children who only attend their homeroom classes.

Curricula for special needs classes vary depending on the ingenuity of each school. But as the students are much bigger and stronger compared to infants, female teachers at times struggle to handle the kids when they try to run away or make a ruckus while rolling on the ground.

In the special needs class we visited in July 1974 in the Tokyo metropolitan area, there were fourteen children, three full-time teachers, and three assistant teachers. However, not all fourteen students come every day, as there are days when they to go to their homeroom class. Thus, the number of children to be taught every day is four to six, and therefore, the ratio between student and teacher is 1:1.

The day we went for a tour was Tuesday. A total of four students were there, including one eight-year-old, two nine-year-old's and one ten-year-old, all of them boys. Two of them were fat like big-bellied sumo wrestlers. The teacher told us that this may be because they eat endless amounts of anything they like....

The teachers there had tried various things, but found physical education to be most beneficial. They placed a lot of emphasis on it, so the students had all changed into gym clothes to do radio exercises or mat exercises. However, none of the children could exercise alone. The teachers had to hold their hands to raise and lower their arms. They could not even do forward rolls adequately, and if one child was doing it, another one would go climb up the slide, and yet another would go climb up the window frame. They each did their separate activities.

One boy requested to play in the water, saying "Pool! Pool!" But when they all changed into their swimsuits and splashed water at each other, he alone was suddenly reluctant to enter the pool. He asked for "Water, water.," while going into the swimming pool, but when the teacher pointed to the faucet and said, "It's right behind you!," he did not know how to drink from it and instead splashed a bucketful of water at it. He could not figure out how to take a drink until his teacher showed him.

Changing clothes was another hard task which they could not do easily by themselves. The more comprehending students could take off their shirt or pants by the teacher's vocal commands, but some of them simply stood still until the teacher eventually helped them get changed. It made me smile when I saw a younger neurotypical child from the other class come to look up at the bigger autistic students and encourage them: "You gotta get changed quickly!"

During mathematics time, one of the students made up problems by himself, answered them, and graded his own work. They were doing two-digit addition and subtraction, but that child seemed to like division and multiplication better. He would randomly recite the multiplication table, such has "Five times nine is forty-five." According to the teachers, he was taught how to systematically round one-digit numbers to two digits so that he can calculate skillfully, but not yet taught how to round two-digit numbers to three. He would need to be taught a new system to grasp this concept. However, as long as he knows how to calculate like this, he will not stand out in his homeroom class as he will quietly be working on his math.

The children could make verbal requests like "Please give me the book." or "Please give me the towel.," but they could not understand requests from others through words alone. The communication is mostly one-directional, so it does not become a conversation.

The children would also pinch and kick other people, but this school did not accept such behavior. Instead, the teacher would pinch and kick the child back. According to the teachers, the arm of one child's mother was red from all the pinching, and his grandmother's skin had gotten so bad it looked as though it had been ripped off. But since his previous schools placed an emphasis on acceptance, they did not punish him for his behavior. But doing so will only propel him to do it to anyone, anywhere, which is why the teachers said they pinch back to teach the children of their bad behavior. This all seemed like rather hard labor.

One teacher also shared that children who have spent time at kindergartens and nursery schools are generally well-developed, while children who have received play therapy, or so-called "treatment," have not developed basic lifestyle habits. There are many children who cannot wash their own face or change their clothes, and some of them do not wash their hair for more than a year so they smell terribly bad. Though some mothers say, "My child cannot wash his face.," or "He cannot wipe his butt.," many children learn to wash their hair when forcibly taken to the tub and splashed with water. They do not learn because the mothers say "they can't" or "it is impossible," so it is better not to coddle the children too much. And while the teacher went on to say, "But, in truth, I believe it might be too late if they have already reached school age. After all, it is said that only about 1% can really adapt well, 20-30% become intellectually disabled, and 50% cannot be helped at all…, " he eagerly continued to teach the children how to round up numbers.

Afterword

The first edition of this book was published in January 1976, which sold 15 times its initial print run. Many newspapers and magazines wrote introductory articles, which resulted in lots of requests for me to examine people's children. Consequently, I opened my personal office "Luna Children's Counseling Center" in Bunkyo ward, Tokyo in 1977, when I was forty years old. Children came from all over Japan, from Hokkaido to Kyushu. But since they lived all over the country, it was difficult to bring them to Tokyo. So, I decided to make business trip consultations for children outside of the Kanto region.

Within a year, the counseling office was providing guidance to about 150 children from Hokkaido in the north to Okinawa in the south. Eight children had already completed treatment without any problems. All of these children were able to behave like other children in kindergarten and elementary school. They had no remnants of their past selves.

However, it takes two or three years to become completely normal, and unfortunately not all children improved. Nonetheless, I was glad that the number of cases that improved in a month increased after adopting new methods such as turning off the night light and setting dietary restrictions introduced in this new edition of my book.

In 2012, I closed my personal office. Over the course of thirty-five years, I treated about 10,000 people and 10% of them improved to the level of neurotypical individuals. They become good workers. Some of them married and had children. Recently, two of them came to meet me. One of them had graduated from university and was going to be a teacher, while the other was a high school student. I was very happy to see them.

Currently, if treatment is started by the age of two or three, there will be much progress by the time the children enter kindergarten at the age of four. They will be close to the level of neurotypical children at least by the time they enter elementary school. Many children have hope.

What is frightening about autism is that children who grow older with it never become "normal." Children who have not learned the language to communicate with others by school age not only do not develop, but in some cases, regression occurs from around the age of ten. Their movement becomes very slow, and they will not even recognize their parents' faces. They may even reach a state of just eating and living.

So far, some of the child psychiatrists and psychological judges who have dealt with a lot of children with autism disagree with my theory, saying "it's a leap" or "television doesn't matter." There are many of these comments, but since the influence of these people is great, we would like to make some achievements as soon as possible and respond to such criticism.

Please try self-treatment.

You can diagnose on your own.

1. The child does not turn around when they are called by

their name.

2. They wander all over the place.
3. They only know a few words by the time they are one-and-a-half years old.

Treatment

4. Cut off all artificial sounds. In particular, turn off the TV for three years.
5. Do not give them much food.
6. Do not give them drinks except water.
7. Do not put them in kindergarten until two years after cutting out the TV.

This treatment is effective until three years of age, and especially so until two-and-a-half years. It is not effective for children over four years. In general, it is still a matter of trial and error, but I would like to continue my research and somehow break down the "age barrier."

Now I am eighty-four years old, live in a retirement village, and have no consultation room. I cannot give you a consultation nor give a lecture.

Last, but not least, I would like to express my sincere gratitude to my publishers for their support in publishing this book, and to the mothers who kindly agreed to provide the data.

December 2021
Kyoko Iwasa

About the Author

Kyoko IWASA

Born in Tokyo in 1937.

Graduated in 1961 from Waseda University Faculty of Letters, Department of Psychology.

Worked as a clinical psychologist at Inokashira Hospital and Yoyogi Hospital.

Currently the Director of Luna Children's Counseling Center.

Engaged in psychological counseling for three-year-old children at the Tokyo Health Center from 1968 to 1977.